Our Legacy

A Testimony to God's Faithfulness

By

3Crosses Church

randy@3crosses.org

Our Legacy: A Testimony to God's Faithfulness/3Crosses Church — 1st ed.

ISBN: _________

DreamCasters Publishing

Acknowledgements

We would like to thank the Legacy Senior Adult community at 3Crosses Church for their participation in this project. The testimonies they have each shared regarding God's faithfulness and provision in their lives are truly inspirational. We also thank the pastoral staff of 3Crosses for their encouragement in this endeavor. To those staff members who assisted with the compilation and publishing of these testimonies on our church website, we express our hearty appreciation.

Contents

Preface

Come my children, listen to me; I will teach you the fear of the Lord.

- PSALM 34:11 NIV

These commandments that I give you today are to be on your hearts. Impress them on your children.

- DEUTERONOMY 6:6 NIV

O God, we have heart with our ears, Our fathers have told us, The work that Thou didst in their days.

- PSALM 44:1 NASB

I was young and now I am old, yet I have not seen the righteous forsaken or their children begging bread.

- PSALM 37:25 NIV

Thy testimonies are also my delight,
They are my counselors.

- PSALM 119:24 NASB

The idea for this project was birthed in a year of great upheaval and challenge. 2020 will be remembered for the outbreak of the Covid-19 pandemic, for sheltering in place, mask mandates, social distancing and lockdowns. As the entire world struggled to cope with a "new normal," so too did the senior adult ministry at 3Crosses Church in Castro Valley, California. We sought to adapt to the new circumstances thrust upon us.

The senior adult ministry had been a rather robust and active group at the beginning of 2020. Several hundred seniors (aged 60 and above) met regularly in-person for prayer, Bible teaching, and fellowship. We met for "Challengers" Sunday school classes and on Thursdays as "Active Adults."

Then the Covid-19 outbreak hit, and by March churches were forced to close and everyone was confined to their homes. In response to this challenge, 3Crosses (along with churches around the world) turned to a technological solution: the online worship service. 3Crosses began streaming their Sunday service and the congregation learned how to log in and participate. This was certainly a less-than-perfect substitute for the face-to-face worship and fellowship experience we were used to, but at least it allowed us some connection with each other as we gathered online to hear the Word of God preached each Sunday.

What of the senior adult ministry, though? Was it just to be shut down until the pandemic was over or were these seniors up to the challenge of embracing new technology so that they could also meet online?

The senior adult leadership team of Pastor Butch Monk, Pastor Randy Odom, Bob and Susan Okamura, Mike Absher, Eric Halverson, and Amy Williams prayed and agreed to consolidate everyone into one group. We would then host

Thursday morning Zoom meetings for Bible teaching, prayer and fellowship. The challenge of trying to teach new computer skills to adults in their 70's, 80's and even 90's was met head on. By God's grace, we succeeded through faith, patience, perseverance, determination and a lot of laughter as young Amy Williams acted as our own personal IT department and call center.

By spring of 2020 the Thursday morning Zoom meeting was up and running and by June, the seniors had the largest, most consistent participation of any of the 3Crosses Zoom meetings! The senior adult ministry had shown themselves to be a vibrant part of the 3Crosses faith community.

It was during this time of change and challenge that the Lord stirred up the leadership team with questions about our purpose and mission. How did the senior adults fit in with the rest of the 3Crosses ministry?

In late July, Eric Halverson shared with the team what he had experienced during his morning prayer and Bible reading time. He had been strongly impressed that it was the duty of the older generation to pass on to the younger generation their personal testimony of how God had been faithful to them all through their lives. He had been led to many Scriptures that supported this idea. Eric then asked the others what they thought about challenging the senior adults to share their testimonies of faith in writing, and then collecting those testimonies in book form. The book could then be made available to younger 3Crosses members and families.

The team wholeheartedly embraced the idea, believing it to be guidance from the Lord. Prior to putting the testimonies in a book, we would begin by posting them on the church website as they were submitted. During this endeavor the theme began to emerge that our senior adults were to provide a legacy for the church. This conviction led the group to brand the senior adult ministry as "Legacy Seniors at 3Crosses."

Those who participated in the project were encouraged to tell their story in their own way with no restrictions or limits on length or written subject matter. While we edited some spelling and grammar, we have published the testimonies essentially how we received them so that each one's unique personality would shine through. Each person's story is truly their story, in their own words.

You will not find the Apostle Paul, Martin Luther, John Calvin or Billy Graham in these pages. These are "ordinary" people. But we pray that you will be encouraged and strengthened in your faith as you see what extraordinary things our wonderful God has done in our ordinary lives!

To God Be the Glory

Great Things He Has Done!

Bob Okamura

The Promise Keeper

My walk with the Lord doesn't seem very long to me, but as I look back on my life, I can see that the hand of God was working on me. He refined my spiritual gifts and skills that He used in my later years.

My life journey began in May of 1942 when I was born in Lodi, California, a small community in the Central Valley between Sacramento and Stockton. My dad was born in Hawaii, but when he was ready to go to school, my grandparents sent him to Japan for his education. He is known as a *kibei*, which means that he was a U.S. citizen, educated in Japan and returned to the US.

My mom was born in Burlingame, California and went to school in the United States. After she graduated from San Mateo Junior College, my grandfather took her to Japan to find her a husband. An arrangement was made for my dad and mom to get married, and the ceremony was performed in the U.S.

A month or two after I was born, our family was ordered to report to the Bay Area for assignment to an internment camp. The United States had entered World War II six months earlier when Japan attacked Pearl Harbor in Hawaii. We ended up in Rower, Arkansas where we spent the next three-and-a-half years.

In 1945, we left camp to go to Chicago, Illinois because my dad found a job there. My brother, Steven, was born there but he lived for only three days. My dad and mom had Rh incompatibility, which means that the first child is born healthy, but their subsequent children have blood disorders. These days, doctors test to see if parents have this condition; if so, they order a complete blood transfusion shortly after birth to save the child. My parents were told that they couldn't have any more children so I grew up as an only child. Several years later, we came back to California on a train and settled in a small farming community known as Acampo, which is located several miles north of Lodi.

We were not a Christian family, at least outwardly. After my mom passed away, I found her baptism certificate from a Baptist Church, something she had never mentioned. Most of my parents' friends were Buddhists. When I was 8 years old, my mom asked me if I wanted to go to a church in Lodi with a classmate's family. I said sure and enjoyed Sunday School, but the church did not emphasize teaching the children about Jesus Christ. After several years, I stopped going and did not attend any church for the next ten years.

After graduating from high school in 1960, I attended UC Berkeley and went to church with several of my classmates. But again, the preaching and teaching didn't emphasize the grace of Jesus and no invitations were given. I got busy with other things and distractions and stopped attending church.

After graduating with a degree in civil engineering, I went to work for the City of Los Angeles. However, the draft board caught up with me and ordered me to take an induction physical exam. I didn't want to be drafted into the Army so I decided to join the Navy reserve. When I went on active duty, I was assigned to a Naval Construction Battalion (a Seabee maintenance unit) and we were deployed in Dong Ha, Vietnam from June 1966 to June 1967. We worked 6-1/2 days a week, with Sunday afternoons off. But we were given the option to go to chapel on Sunday morning, and a lot of guys went just to get out of working in the morning. I went because some of my friends asked me to go with them. It was a multi-denominational service because there was only one chaplain and one service each Sunday. I still didn't know what it meant to be a Christian.

After returning from Vietnam in June of 1967, I was separated from active duty and went to work. I got married in 1970 and we had one daughter. I worked for various government agencies and private engineering companies, gradually developing my skills and working my way up the corporate ladder. Unfortunately, the marriage did not work out and I found myself pursuing worldly things.

During that time, I went to several churches, searching for something to give me direction in my life. One day in February 1992, I felt particularly empty and alone. So, I decided to call Neighborhood Church, where I had attended once before with a friend, and asked to talk to a pastor. I met with Rev. Malcolm Cash who spent several hours explaining the Gospel to me. After he was done, he asked me if I wanted to accept Jesus as my Lord and Savior, and I said yes.

After I accepted Jesus as my Lord, I had many questions about what that meant. So, I began reading an old King James Bible that my mother had given me back in 1950. As I read, I came across a passage that really piqued my interest. St. Matthew 10:38 reads, "And he that taketh not his cross, and followeth after me, is not worthy of me." As a new Christian, I didn't know what that meant so I kept reading, wanting to learn what that passage was telling me. Then I came to St. John 12:26 which says, "If any man serve me, let him follow me; and where I am, there shall also my servant be; if any man serve me, him will my Father honour."

The Holy Spirit opened my eyes and I knew I was to obey God's teachings and serve Him. That started my path to God's service. I volunteered to becomes an usher because I felt that was the only thing I could do as a baby Christian.

My mountain top experience came in June 1992 when I went to a Promise Keeper's conference in Boulder, Colorado. The event was held in the Colorado Buffaloes football stadium with approxi-mately 35,000 men in attendance. We sang praises to God and heard two days of inspiring messages. That awe-inspiring moment lit a fire in me to go back to Neighborhood Church and begin searching for a way to serve.

I worked in the singles ministry and the usher's ministry, where I eventually became the Head Usher and served for 14 years. I was then approached to serve on the Governing Elders Board for a period of time. In 1993, Promise Keepers brought one of their conferences to the Oakland Coliseum and I volunteered to work in the hospitality area. The conference returned to the Coliseum in 1994 and I was chosen to be the event manager. I was put in charge of the entire event as a volunteer, which was quite an honor.

In 2005, I had the opportunity to go on two short term missions trips with Foot Steps, a missions organization, and was able to use my gift of administration to help the others do their work. I went to Romania to help college students with church repair work and evangelized the local residents of Timisoara. I also helped a women's group conduct Vacation Bible School classes in Sibiu. In 2006 I led a group to Costa Rica to teach Vacation Bible School classes and witness to the local residents of Puerto Viejo de Sarapiqui. We also did extensive church repair work in the capital of San Jose. In 2009 I had the opportunity to go to Cambodia to use my engineering skills to help design a plan for a private university site in Kampong Chhnang.

After I retired in 2007, I volunteered to help with administration work in the senior adult ministry. Eventually I came on staff to work in the senior adult ministry and the finance office. I used my construction and administration skills to coordinate church activities with the general contractor and the architect for the remodel of the A, B and C classrooms, the work on the Children's Ministry Center and the relocation of the Chapel. Several years later, I did the coordination work for the construction of the Connection Center/Café 4 building.

As I look back on my life, I can see where God had His hand on me as I developed skills that I would use when I became a believer. My main spiritual gift is administration and God used that gift in the usher, singles, senior adult and missions ministries and also during church construction work. My current job title is Missions and Senior Adult Ministry Coordinator.

God brought Susan to be my wife and, together, this wonderful woman and I serve on staff at 3Crosses, using our gifts, talents and skills to do what God has called us to do.

I became a Christian at age 50, so there is always hope for those in your family circle, co-workers and friends, no matter how old they are. Keep praying for grandparents, parents, siblings, friends and co-workers.

Key Scriptures

In addition to Matthew 10:28 and John 12:26, there are two other verses which mean a lot to me. The first is Hebrews 13:5, which reads, "Keep your lives free from the love of money and be content with what you have, because God has said, 'Never will I leave you; never will I forsake you.'" That verse keeps me focused on God rather than my own needs or wants.

The second is 1 Corinthians 13:13, which so many people recite. "And now these remain: faith, hope and love. But the greatest of these is love." This verse keeps me focused on others and not myself.

Brenda Nelson

Humpty Dumpty Sat on a Wall

My first time in a church, I was 4 years old. My mother, stepfather and I were living temporarily with my grand-mother in Brooklyn, New York. My mother did not go to church, so my grandmother asked her if she could take me. She and I walked across town to this white steepled Christian church. On the way my grandmother introduced me to the butcher, baker and everyone she knew on the way. I never felt so special and loved.

When it came time to sing the hymns, everyone picked up their hymnal books and began singing. I wanted to join them but I didn't know how to read. So I said to myself, "I will open the book and sing along and no one will know I can't read." I sang all my nursery rhymes as loud as I could.

"Humpty Dumpty sat on a wall."

"Little Miss Muffet sat on a tuffet."

"Baa Baa black sheep have you any wool?"

My grandmother let me sing and never asked me to be quiet. I felt so good that when we left the church I thought I want THAT in my life!

During the month that we lived with my grandmother she also taught me the Lord's Prayer and "Now I lay me down to sleep." She would tuck me in at night and sit on my bed while I said my prayers. At the end of the month we left and moved many times, including out of state. I would often ask my mother if we could go to church but she always said no. I asked her if she would ask a neighbor who went to church if they would take me. She said yes and would, wherever we moved.

When I was nine years old, my grandmother sent me a Bible and I was thrilled. I didn't understand the King James Version but said to myself, "someday I will." As I grew up, I searched for a church. As a teenager, I went by myself to a variety of small churches but no one ever acknowledged that I was there. It was a very lonesome feeling.

I eventually married an Oakland policeman and we had two children. We were living in Castro Valley in 1974 and on Mother's Day he asked me what I wanted to do. I told him I wanted to go to Neighborhood Church, the one with the three crosses in front. We took our young children and I prayed that someone would greet us with a smile.

Frida Post, my first church friend, greeted us with a big smile and welcomed us to Neighborhood Church. That was it! My children would grow up in the church and my husband and I became active members before he died in 2003. Our whole family invited Jesus into our hearts in 1974 when Pastor Bellig was leading the church.

We all immediately joined a Sunday school class, and with the excellent Bible teaching at Neighborhood, I grew to understand the Bible my grandmother had given to me when I was only nine.

My husband and I hosted a Tuesday night Bible study for 30 years, and it has continued even after his death. The blessing of my grandmother taking me to church and letting me sing "Humpty Dumpty" has led my two children, four grandchildren, and six great-grandchildren to be strong Christians who are walking in step with the Lord.

BUTCH MONK

From Sky Pilot to Challenger

I was born into a Christian family and regularly atten-ded Havenscourt Colonial church in Oakland. Each Sunday was a family affair with no questions asked; church atten-dance was required. Church included morning and evening worship along with Sunday School, Junior Church, and weeknight meetings.

Each Sunday was a church day through and through, with no wearing of play clothes or going outside after church. In fact, the only outing allowed after church was an afternoon ride with the family while we all listened to the radio. Now-legendary radio entertainment including "Fibber McGee and Molly" or "The Jack Benny Show" was considered acceptable listening on the Sunday ride.

Even throughout the week, our activities were pre-dominantly church-oriented. I participated in the "Sky Pilots" each week where we learned memory verses, worked on model planes and even took boxing lessons. My parents participated in many church activities from singing in the choir, to leading songs in an adult Sunday school class to cooking for church events. The significance for me in all of this was the development of a church-oriented mindset where all scheduling of activities hinged on what was happening at church.

One Sunday morning after Junior Church, my two older sisters took me to listen to the missionary guest speaker in order for me to have a personal conversation about what it meant to "give my heart to Jesus." I am not sure about my motivation for listening to this presentation. It was probably a mixture of fear and curiosity, along with the fact that everybody else was doing it. I usually did what my sisters asked and I knew that my parents would be happy that I finally "made a decision" to follow Christ. While sitting on the steps to the Junior Church room, I prayed to accept Christ and began my journey as a follower of Jesus.

Shortly thereafter, my parents decided that it was time to take their family to Neighborhood Church of Oakland. Neighborhood offered many more children's and youth programs, along with a dynamic music ministry and an evangelistic emphasis on the local community and the world. Jake Bellig was the pastor, whose goal was to reach the Bay Area for Christ. Every Sunday night, Pastor Jake and a group of dedicated volunteers presented illustrated sermons that were titled after modern songs. I found each service to be a fascinating combination of biblical history and contem-porary application. I was in high school at the time and it was during one of those services that I rededicated myself to truly following Jesus.

I started teaching in the junior high school department when I was eighteen years old. Ed Harris Sr. and his wife provided an inviting atmosphere with strong biblical teaching and fun outings like ice skating to trips to Santa Cruz and summer camp. The group kept growing and became a focal point for all my activities, just as I had experienced as a youngster. The church moved to its Castro Valley location in 1969 and the junior high ministry continued it growth. We began to use the gym each week for Sunday School and break out classes that required movable partitions to be put up each week.

When Ed asked for someone to coach a girl's basketball team, Pat Cozzens and I volunteered to take on the job. It was during this time when I realized that Pat was the girl for me. I proposed after one of those basketball practices and we were married in August of 1970. By this time, I was teaching English at St. Felicitas Catholic School so the audience for our wedding was a batch of students from St. Felicitas and another group from our Junior High group at Neighborhood Church.

In all of these events, I could see God's divine hand of provi-dence working on my behalf. None of the events were accidental or coincidental. God certainly had orchestrated each event, from childhood to young adulthood, with His own special purposes in mind. I became the director of the Junior High department in the mid-1970s and became a part-time staff member in 1975.

In 1972 I left St. Felicitas and moved to Redwood Christian School where I again taught English and eventually became a part of the administrative team. A new campus was opened at Neigh-borhood Church in September of 1975, and I was named principal. I retired from Redwood Christian School in 2008. During these years, working at both the church and school, I had many opportunities to see God work in the lives of individuals and families. I have had the privilege of being part of countless programs and ministry opportunities all because God lovingly showed me grace and allowed me to be a means by which His work could be accomplished.

In December of 1990, I began to teach adults for the first time, becoming the teacher of the Challenger's class. This class has become a major blessing that has led to many other opportunities, including Active Adults on Thursdays. God has blessed Pat and me with an exciting ministry, four children, fifteen grandchildren, and innumerable Christian friends who have been our support system throughout the years. I thank the Lord for the influence of my parents and two Bible-believing churches that consistently taught God's Word, provided opportunities and accepted the many bumps in the road along the way.

Thoughts for the Next Generation

First of all, I would advise any young believer to make a daily quiet time with the Lord an absolute, consistent priority. In the midst of balancing two jobs and the busyness of life, God has used the daily quiet time as the means for providing daily guidance and wisdom for my larger lifetime decisions.

Secondly, I would advise the young believers of the next generation to make an absolute surrendered effort to organize their lives around Jesus Christ. When decisions are to be made, and relationships developed, it is absolutely essential that one put Christ and the principles of His Word first and foremost. Often, we think that the hurried, busy life that the world requires is somehow a sign of influence and status. But, as we commit ourselves to the Lord, we find that making Him the center of life, and slowing down to linger with Him daily in prayer are the keys to success as believers.

Finally, I have learned that strong Christian friends are an absolute joy and necessity for living the Christian life. Having a few, close friends with whom you can share perspectives, problems, and prayer will prove to be just what is needed when one becomes entangled in the difficulties of this world.

Key Scriptures

Trust in the Lord with all your heart and lean not on your own under-standing; in all your ways submit to him, and he will make your paths straight.

- PROVERBS 3:5-6

As a prisoner for the Lord, then, I urge you to live a life worthy of the calling you have received...one God and Father of all, who is over all and through all and in all.

- EPHESIANS 4:1, 6

But the wisdom that comes from heaven is first of all pure; then peace-loving, considerate, submissive, full of mercy and good fruit, impartial and sincere. Peacemakers who sow in peace reap a harvest of righteousness.

- JAMES 3:17-18

Carl Anderson

Begin the Day with Prayer

Around the time I was born, my mother had a dream that she had died and tried to gain access into Heaven, but God would not admit her. Based on this experience, she decided to return to church and take her children, too. Consequently, I began attending a Christ-centered church at a young age, and at approximately the age of 9, I accepted Christ as my Savior.

Now that I am older, this is what I would like to share with the next generation. I firmly believe that prayer and Bible study are integral parts of the Christian life and need to be practiced daily to strengthen one's faith. Praying allows us to stay close to God and is necessary for confessing sin and obtaining forgiveness. It is an indication that we are relying on God for wisdom and not trying to live the Christian life on our own power, something that is impossible to do.

God's standards are high, but through prayer, we can grow spiritually and take on more of the nature of Jesus Christ.

Reading and studying God's Word will also transform our thoughts, words and deeds to be pleasing to God. His Word is full of guidance that will improve our lives and those of others as well.

Memorizing scripture is a worthwhile endeavor as you will have it readily available when facing temptation or life's challenges. If I neglect prayer and Bible study, my spiritual life suffers. Conversely, beginning the day with prayer and the reading of His Word gives me comfort and strength.

Key Scripture

One of my favorite Bible verses is a commandment given by Christ in Matthew 7:12 of the King James Version: "Therefore all things whatsoever that ye would that men would do to you, do ye even so to them: for this is the law and the prophets.

This instruction sums up how to live according to the Spirit. Jesus is telling us to treat others as we would want them to treat us. By following His perfect example, we will improve our relation-ships with others and possibly give them hope.

Bob Ryan

Port O'Call

Bob was 17 years old, and lived in small town Lubbock, Texas with his family. He had been raised in a Southern Baptist Church but he was making plans to go out with a group of friends to rob a school house. Previously, they had broken into a bakery and stolen some pies.

But that night his mom wanted him to go to a tent revival meeting at church. Bob planned on going for a short while and then leaving to join the other teenager. His stepfather, who was on crutches because of a foot injury, watched him go into the tent meeting. Bob's plan to run away and meet his friends failed because his stepfather was watching him to make sure that he stayed at the tent meeting. That night, Bob heard the gospel message and went forward to accept the Lord. His life was completely changed!

While this was happening, his friends were caught and arrested while trying to break into the school house. The judge gave them the choice to go to jail or join the Army and be sent to the front lines of the Korean War. Every one of the friends chose jail except for one young man who joined the Army and was later saved by Christ. He died a hero's death on the front lines; while guarding the other soldiers, he wiped out a whole squadron of attacking Korean soldiers. He died with his machine gun in his arms.

Bob went on to college, then was ordained as a pastor in the Southern Baptist Convention. He was later drafted into the U.S. Navy and served once again in the Korean war. He visited the Neighborhood Church's Port O'Call in Oakland. That's where he met his wife, Diane, who was a Port O' Call hostess. They were married at Neighborhood Church by Dr. Jacob Bellig.

Neighborhood Church moved to Castro Valley, where Bob taught Sunday school for several years, sang in the church choir and enjoyed his time as a church greeter.

Cindy Viada

The Lord is My Shepherd

My mother became very ill in 1983, when I was only 21 years old. She was in a coma in a hospital when I prayed, "God if you are real, take my mother home." Fifteen or so minutes later God answered my prayer.

One year later, in December 1984, I came to 3Crosses to watch a Christmas performance. At the end, the pastor asked if anyone wanted to receive Jesus Christ as their Lord and Savior, so I raised my hand and went to the prayer room. One of the pastors read the Four Spiritual Laws to me and that was when I asked Jesus into my heart.

My walk with the Lord and my faith became stronger. I'm able to do a lot for God now because I listen more and read Scripture. God's love is so strong that I can tune in to Him each day, and through His Holy Spirit, He shows me more of who He is.

When I was younger in my faith, I did not really understand who God was. Thirty years later, my faith has grown and, with people praying for me, God moved me to a better place to live. Now I am obeying God and helping more people at church as a member of the First Aid team.

I know God can help anyone who wants to receive His son Jesus Christ as their Lord and Savior. He is a loving God, always caring, and always here. He is also a healing God who gives you serenity everyday. He will never leave you nor forsake you. When you have Jesus in your life, you are never truly alone, even when it seems so. No one can take you from God's hands, nor can you get out of His hands. God loves you no matter who you are or your background.

You are joining a really big family when you become a Christian but it is not an easy road. There are many trials, tribulations, mountains and valleys but you have eternal life and will be with Jesus in Heaven someday. Forever, there will be no more crying, no more pain and no more death. Jesus wants everyone to be saved. Join His family today, for Jesus will give you real peace, not man's peace, but God's peace. His arms are open wide for all to come to Him.

Key Scripture

My favorite Bible verse is from Psalm 23. "The Lord is my shepherd, I shall not want." God gives me what I need all the time. I do not need to worry about anything at all because He always provides for all my needs. I pray daily and God covers my needs.

Dave Rogers

Godly Parents Create a Legacy

My journey with Jesus began at a very young age as I was born into a Christ centered family. In my early years my dad helped set up evangelical tent meetings with sawdust trails. We had family devotions every Saturday morning, then went to church every Sunday morning and again on Sunday night.

I was led to the Lord by my mother when she asked me if I wanted to go to heaven. I said, "Yes," and accepted Jesus into my heart. From that time on, with guidance from my parents, I followed the Lord and experienced all His blessings.

My dad was my Sunday School Teacher. Through the Sky Pilots Organization (a Boys Scout type program), we built model airplanes and flew them at parks and schools on the weekends to attract people who we could share the gospel with. I crashed almost all of my planes but it was one of many special connections that I had with my dad.

My story isn't dramatic; it is just the opposite and somewhat anti-climactic. The reason for writing it is to share how the Lord has blessed me through my godly parents and home. My parents shared their beliefs with me and modeled them as well. Their walk matched their talk. What they did convinced me that this is how Christian parents should raise their children. My dad spent quality (and quantity) time with me in scripture memorization, witnessing, Bible reading, going to Mount Hermon, and attending Gideon and Christian Business Men (CBMC) meetings, as well as many work and fun activities.

As I grew up, I learned to trust the Lord to help me in school. Studying wasn't my favorite thing and I really disliked homework but with the Lord's help I got through school. My mom and dad wanted me to go to college and encouraged me to attend Biola University. Attending Biola was one of the best experiences of my life. I matured from a shy introverted child into a young man who became Sophomore Class President and Student Body Athletic Director (I got to choose the cheerleaders). I also played basketball and ran track. By taking 25 semester credits of Bible classes at Biola, I gained a solid understanding of the scriptures.

On one of our basketball trips from Biola to the Bay Area, two of my teammates stayed at my home for a couple of nights. On the bus trip back to school, the coach asked each member of the team about their favorite part of the trip. To my surprise, my two teammates said that staying at my house and meeting my parents was their favorite part. From this, I began to understand how special my parents were and how unique my home and upbringing were.

My aunt, sister and cousins worked on the summer staff at Mount Hermon so I applied for a staff job and was accepted.

I spent the next four summers working as the baker. During those summers I attended many of the conferences and heard some of the leading Christian speakers. My third summer was when I met my future wife. We ran into some rough patches during our dating so I wrote a letter to my folks seeking their advice. A couple of days later, to my surprise, they came up to Mount Hermon. I asked them what they were doing there and my dad said, "you asked for some advice so we wanted to pray with you in person to seek His guidance."

We were married for 14 years and had two daughters but the marriage eventually ended in divorce. But the breakup provided me with the opportunity to grow closer to the Lord. When you go through a trauma and have everything taken away from you, that's when you hold on tight to whatever gives you stability. The Lord was faithful and provided supportive friends and family who helped me though that turbulent time.

I continued coming to Neighborhood Church (3Crosses) and eventually joined the Singles Class. By being where the Lord wanted me, I met my future wife, Linda, who was widowed. We have a daughter who grew up in the church and continues to be a Christ-follower. We've been married for 37 years and the Lord couldn't have provided a better partner and companion.

My dad died when I was 24 and in my last year of graduate school. The night I left his hospital bed, I knew I might never see him again. Although I did lose him, I would never lose the precious memories that he had created for me.

It was easy to see how God the Father is a God of love because I had an earthly Father who constantly showed me how much he loved me. Two years later my mother married a George Clooney look-alike who was just as godly and just as loving as my father. I was blessed by having three loving fathers (the Lord, my dad, and my step-dad).

My parents gave me a legacy of following Christ and enjoying his fellowship, a legacy that has sustained me through these past 76 years. He has blessed me more than I can ever imagine and I am looking forward to spending eternity with Him.

I wrote this testimony, having been convicted during the night that I should write something about my Christian family upbringing. I read this passage in the Billy Graham devotional "Unto the Hills":

I want to suggest Ten Commandments for a solid happy God-honoring home:

1. Establish God's chain of command. The Bible teaches that for the Christian, Jesus Christ is to head the home, with the wife under the authority of a Christ-like husband and the children responsible to their parents.
2. Obey the commandments to love one another.
3. Show acceptance and appreciation for each family member.
4. Family members should respect God's authority over them and the authority God has delegated down the chain of command.
5. It is important to have training and discipline in the home and not just for the family dog.
6. Enjoy one another and take time to enjoy family life together. Quality time is not a substitute for quantity time. Quantity time is quality time.
7. Do not commit adultery. Adultery destroys a marriage and is a sin against God and against your mate.
8. Everyone in a family should work for the mutual benefit of the family. No child should be without chores or

without the knowledge that work brings fulfillment.

9. Pray together and read the Bible together. Nothing strengthens a marriage and family more. Nothing is a better defense against Satan.
10. Every family member should be concerned about whether every other member of the family is truly saved. This extends after the immediate family to grandparents, uncles, and aunts, cousins and in-laws.

Key Scripture

"My son, do not forget my teaching, but keep my commands in your heart, for they will prolong your life many years and bring you peace and prosperity. Let love and faithfulness never leave you; bind them around your neck, write them on the tablet of your heart. Then you will win favor and a good name in the sight of God and man. Trust in the Lord with all your heart and lean not on your own understanding; in all your ways submit to him, and he will make your paths straight."

- PROVERBS 3:1-6

David Morrow

New Blessings Every Day

I was born in Maud, Oklahoma on June 5, 1933. My father, Joseph, had moved there from Texas and my mother Florence (Ritchie) Morrow had come from Arkansas. My father was a poor (but honest) carpenter/farmer, as were so many Americans who were struggling to survive during the time of the Great Depression. To make matters worse, the State of Oklahoma, which had held out so much promise to homesteading settlers, was plagued by huge dust storms in the 1930's, which became increasingly severe each year. Devastation of the land was followed by bankruptcies, which swept across the land. You would find it interesting to learn more about that phenomenon.

My father took Mother and me to the beckoning land of California to find work when I was four. The climate and air agreed so much more with Mother that we soon migrated to the Central Valley of California. John Steinbeck wrote a famous book called "The Grapes of Wrath," which describes the great migration of poor people like our family to California.

We settled in Turlock and in time Dad was able to buy twenty acres with a small, one bedroom house. He acquired a small bunkhouse from the neighbor across the road and pulled it onto our property. Although it had no water or heat, it provided sleeping quarters for my brother, Don, and me until I went away to college.

I was always busy as a boy. We had cows to milk, eggs to collect and wood to chop. About a quarter of our twenty acres were planted in eucalyptus trees and Dad, Don and I spent much of our "spare" time chopping down the trees to clear the land and cutting up the wood to sell.

A neighbor who lived beyond us stopped by and gave me a ride to school with his sons. Another nearby neighbor family invited me to ride with their family to attend Vacation Bible School, and it was at this time that I was introduced to Christ and accepted Him as my Savior. The VBS was run by the American Sunday School Union, an organization that I am grateful for and have continued to support to this day, as it was through their ministry that I found Christ. Finding Christ was the most significant event of my life. I began attending the little country church with these neighbors and in time my parents began attending and accepted Christ also.

At Modesto Junior College I joined Intervarsity Christian Fellowship, an excellent organization which contributed greatly to my Christian growth. I became president of the group. When they went on a two week camping trip to a remote part of Catalina Island during the summer, I could only go for one week, as I had to work to save money for my next semester.

I completed my undergraduate education at Fresno State College (now California State University at Fresno), where I majored in Social Science, which consisted of Economics, History and Sociology. Again I was involved with Intervarsity, and it was there that I met Beverly Camp. Bev played piano for Intervarsity and somehow I found myself leading the singing! Before I left for graduate school Bev and I were engaged.

I was fortunate to obtain a full scholarship through the Ford Foundation to attend the one year graduate program at San Francisco State College (now University) to become a teacher. Through my church I was put in touch with a family near the college who rented me a room inexpensively, and because of my scholarship and all of my summer jobs—picking peaches, grading them, working in the cannery and going door to door selling Watkins products—I graduated debt free (but flat broke!)

Bev and I were married after I graduated, on July 6, 1956. One month later I was drafted into the Army and had to leave for basic training at Fort Lewis, Washington. Bev was able to join me after six months and my military assignment kept me at Fort Lewis the entire duration of my active duty. Our first child, Francine, was born in Washington.

After my tour of duty ended I was hired as a high school history teacher in Ceres, where I became head of the department. While in Ceres our family attended Mountain View church seven to eight miles west of Turlock. There I assisted in the leadership of the church as Chairman of the Board of Deacons.

Tragedy struck our family while we were there when our first born son, Stephen, died of sudden infant death syndrome at approximately the age of two weeks. Stephen is buried in the children's area of the Ceres Cemetery, near my parents. Bev is also buried there, as I will be.

In Ceres we had a team teaching approach and when I applied for a teaching job in the Bay Area, my experience in team teaching (and also as department head) were the two factors which resulted in my getting a job. After a year at the old Foothill High School in Hayward, I was transferred to the brand new Marina High School in San Leandro. I was there from the day it opened until it closed eighteen years later.

During my time at Marina I continued my education, obtaining two masters' degrees: one in Education and the other in Counseling. Subsequent teaching at Arroyo High School in San Lorenzo and at the San Leandro Adult School rounded out my working years.

Our family attended First American Baptist Church in Hayward, where I was Moderator of the Board of Deacons. Beverly was in charge of Christian Education. To facilitate spiritual depth and provide an opportunity for interaction and support among the members, Bev and I began a small group Bible study in our home, which we led for many years. In 1977 we realized the programs of the church were inadequate for our children, so we began attending the Neighborhood Church (now 3Crosses Church) in Castro Valley. They had a many-faceted, robust youth program, which we felt would be a better fit for our family. I continue to attend that church to this day.

Almost incomprehensibly, our second son, Tim, died in his sleep at the age of 50. Now I had lost two sons. The grief I experienced from this loss, and continue to experience, would be unbearable without the assurance from the Lord that I will see my sons again.

A year later, after a very fulfilling marriage of 57 years, my dear wife, Beverly, succumbed to Alzheimer's, a condition which had plagued her for ten years. My widowed brother, Don, moved in with me. I was grateful that I still had my daughter Francine, son Brian, and daughter-in-law Jane and their families.

Even though my life seemed over, much to my amazement, God brought Jean Braine into my life. Bev and I and Jean and Ray had been friends for many years, having met at Neighborhood Church in the late 70s. Ray died the year following Bev's death, and somehow God orchestrated that Jean and I spend some time together. I had briefly helped care for Ray in his last months and Jean and I had some business dealings together. We were both members of the Gideons, as well as the Challengers adult Sunday School class. Everyone was surprised, including us, when we were married in May of 2015. Our marriage has been such a blessing for both of us!

Serving God in any way I can has always been important to me. One of the prominent values I have had throughout life has been to cherish the friends and family God has given me. A manifestation of this value has been the fact that, along with my wife, I have kept in touch with many people that we met along the way, going all the way back to grade school. For many years Bev and I attended the annual Ritchie family reunion in Oklahoma. It has only been a few years now since those ended. I still have friends whom I made from grade school all the way through high school. Our annual Turlock High School class reunion, when I see some of these dear friends, is a highlight of my year. Each church we attended added a wealth of new friends whom I still treasure and try to maintain contact with. Friends and family are among my most valuable possessions.

Key Scripture

God never promised that life would be easy. In fact, Christ told us to expect that life would be hard. But He did promise never to leave us. And He has been true to His Word. I can say with the Psalmist "The Lord is my strength and song, and He has become my salvation."

- PSALM 118:14

A passage that has been so meaningful to me throughout my life is Proverbs 3:5-6. "Trust in the Lord with all thine heart; and lean not unto thine own understanding. In all thy ways acknowledge him, and he shall direct thy paths." Looking back over my long life of trusting in the Lord, I can attest to His faithfulness to me.

To those who come after me I would say receive Christ early in life, as soon as you learn about Him. Then follow Him where He leads you. Look for His direction, and He will not just lead you but be right with you all along life's difficult journey. With Him, you can handle whatever comes your way.

Debbie Ryan-Zacharoff

Prayers to an Open Heaven

I went to Neighborhood Church in Castro Valley as a child and attended Children's church, where Ed Hubbard was the director.

When I was six years old I had a medical emergency; a fast-acting staph germ and infection stopped my breathing. My dad found me in my bed, all blue in the face, and not breathing. He called the Fire Department and they sent the paramedics to resuscitate me. The Fire Chief rushed me to St. Rose Hospital in Hayward, CA. The doctors said that they had to operate on me. It wasn't quite emergency surgery, but it was close! The doctors gave me a tracheostomy to open up my airways.

I then had an out of body experience! I was totally knocked out for the surgery and not able to breathe on my own but I felt myself floating above the operating table towards the bright lights. I looked down and saw the surgeon and nurses operating on me. I was embarrassed because all I had on were some blue shorts. Soon they resuscitated me and the next thing I remember was waking up in an oxygen tent in the hospital.

As soon as I woke up, a beautiful blonde nurse came over and told me, "Happy Halloween!" She gave me a yellow plastic kitty cat and told me that my brothers and sisters were trick or treating for me that night and were going to save a big orange pumpkin full of candy for me!

I thought about that experience for several years. Then one night, when I was 8 years old, while I was praying to God, I started crying. I felt like my prayers were hitting the bedroom ceiling, and coming back down again! Then my mom came in and asked me, "Debbie, why are you crying?" I told her how I was feeling and she gave me some Bible verses, including John 3:16, and then asked me if I wanted to invite Jesus Christ in my heart. I said, “yes" and right there, my mom prayed with me to receive Christ as my Savior!

At my senior high school church camp meeting at Mt. Hermon, I committed my life to follow God wherever he wanted to lead me. Ron Story, the youth pastor, gave the altar call, which was, "Here I am, Lord, send me."

I attended San Diego Christian College in El Cajon, CA, where I met my husband, Peter. I majored in Education and taught at Redwood Christian Schools, Fremont Christian School, and now I am a 5th grade teacher in a public school.

Key Scriptures

I love to share what the Lord has done for me. Since I received Jesus, I have never had that feeling of my prayers being blocked. Now, I know that Romans 3:23 is true: “For all have sinned, and come short of the glory of God.” However, 1 John 1:9 says; “If we confess our sins, he is faithful and just to forgive us our sins, and cleanse us from all unrighteousness."

Delores Jackson

God Cares

I was one of six children brought up with religion, right and wrong, by godly parents. We even prayed together every night but I never realized Jesus had died on the cross for me. I felt that I never fit in with others so I prayed to God often.

After marriage and the raising of two children, I went through a divorce and really felt insecure. A friend invited me to go to a "prayer circle" with her. Their prayers were what I felt for my life and that's when I asked Jesus into my life.

Key Scripture

Life brought more good and hard times; marriage, death and cancer. But with the Lord's help, I claimed Proverbs 3:5-6: "Trust in the Lord with all your heart, and lean not on your own understanding. In all your ways acknowledge Him, and

He will make your paths straight."

God cares.

Trust Him in all you do.

Stay with God's word.

Diane Ryan

My Heart, Christ's Home

Diane attended First Presbyterian Church in Berkeley under Pastor Robert Boyd Munger who was the author of the pamphlet, "My Heart - Christ's Home." She thought she was a long-time Christian, having attended First Christian Church in Oakland as a child.

One Labor Day weekend there was a Youth Group Retreat at Mt. Hermon that everyone at her church was going to. Diane had decided not to go because she had something else going on that weekend but her girlfriend had everyone call to convince her to go. She finally relented and went to the retreat. There was a Christian speaker there, a surgeon who spoke about being a Christian and related it to medical things. Diane related to that, since she worked at Merritt Hospital in Oakland as an admittance clerk.

The surgeon's wife was ready to have a baby, so everyone was sitting on eggshells while he delivered several messages.

Diane was inspired to go forward and accept the Lord at the retreat. The surgeon left on Sunday morning because his wife finally had the baby.

Diane went to serve as a hostess in the Port O' Call at Neighborhood Church in Oakland. She met a Navy sailor named Bob there. They fell in love and were married at 3Crosses and raised their six kids in the church.

Diane went on to become a nurse LVN and worked at St. Rose and Kaiser Hospitals for more than 35 years. Diane and Bob's kids are all Christians. She served in the Children's Sunday School at Neighborhood Church for more than 60 years. They now enjoy attending the newly renamed Legacy Class.

Dietmar Barnikel

Mercy, Grace and Forgiveness

I think the Lord has always been after me but I've taken a varied path in my faith walk. While growing up in a Christian home in Augsburg, Germany, Hitler's rise to power was the first to sidetrack my walk.

My father was a pastor at our Methodist church, so our family regularly attended Sunday service and school. When I was about 10, I became involved with the "Hitler Youth." Their activities not only conflicted with Sunday worship and study, but also brainwashed us into the Nazi system.

In the beginning, I liked it because of the sports-oriented activities, such as running, hiking and wrestling. I remember that if you did well in your studies, your reward was a picture of a German general from the frontlines. We were told that our "V-1" and V-2" rockets (leading technology at the time) would win the war for us. Of course, that didn't happen.

After the war, at age 14, I had to go to work and landed a job as a confectioner's apprentice. Soon I was entrenched in the restaurant field where the long hours and pursuit of my trade took me on a path away from faithful worship. At this time one of my childhood Bible memory verses, Matthew 11:28, gave me some comfort: "Come to me all you who are weary and burdened and I will give you rest."

My trail led me to work first in Germany, then Switzerland, and then Holland where I took a job on a cruise ship that circled the world. By my mid-twenties, with many travels behind me and more to come, I immigrated to the United States in New York. While there for just 18 months, I was drafted into the U.S. Army and was soon stationed in Okinawa, Japan. While there, I had Sundays off so I again went to church, joined the choir, and met a girl, but that's another story.

After military service, like many immigrants, my path took me in pursuit of the "American Dream." Now in my 30s, I was working Sundays again at country clubs or hotel restaurants in the SF Bay Area. I bought a house, got married, had two kids, moved to Half Moon Bay and pursued what I thought was success. Looking back at those 12 years, I see that my idols were career and money and providing for my family, but not spending the time with them that I should. Before long my life collapsed when my wife began a divorce process. I wanted to quit it all, take a camper and hit the road on a new path.

Worried about my state of mind, my sister in Germany recommended I talk to Robert Wattles, a man she had befriended while he was working with the Navigators organization in Germany after the war and who now lived in the Bay Area. This I did and he shared the Lord with me, giving me Bible verses such as Revelation 3:20: "Here I am! I stand at the door and knock. If anyone hears my voice and opens the door, I will come in and eat with that person, and they with me." I realized that the meal Revelation spoke about was like none I'd ever prepared, but rather, with the Lord, it would entail mercy, grace and forgiveness—just what I needed. Bob and I have remained friends to this day.

On April 13, 1979, I was camping alone on Mount Diablo and struggling with making the commitment to give my life to the Lord. With God's grace, I opened my heart and when I came off the mountain, I met with Robert and told him of my new commitment. He welcomed me and, because I had nowhere else to go, he let me stay with him. He then set me up working as a chef at a Navigators' conference center in Colorado. While working there, I participated in a discipleship program offered to the workers.

I stayed with the Navigators for 3 years and shortly after the program ended, enrolled in Multnomah Bible School in Portland, OR, where I graduated after 3 years. During that time, I was living off of savings and investments and working summers with my son, Eric, at a beautiful resort on the Oregon coast. At this time I felt the Lord leading me to serve Him in China, so I accepted an opportunity to join the Board of Directors at Educational Resources and Referrals China, a mission organization in Berkeley, CA. I was with them for 5 years and was where I met my wife, Marty, who was Assistant Director in charge of recruiting and training Christians to go to China to teach English.

In 1991 they arranged for me to visit many parts of China as a chef consultant/teacher and visit ERRC teachers to see how I could help out. This was just after the Tiananmen square incident so the hotel and tourist business was down. Nothing long-term developed for me, so I ended up going around the world again, this time by plane and train, consulting and working along the way.

After I returned from my travels, Marty and I began our courtship and in October 1993 we were married. I still had to work many Sundays but I regularly attended weekly Bible studies. In 2007, we found ourselves at 3Crosses, taking the 101 class and that's where I learned about, and started the very rewarding discipline of a daily quiet time. This habit has really helped me grow spiritually along with the great spiritual influence Marty has had on me. Our life together is an adventure in which we challenge each other, pray and do devotions together. While at 3Crosses, we have been involved in International Student Fellowship, which has met our desire to reach internationals for Christ without going overseas. I have also been involved in CrossStreets ministry, primarily an outreach to local people in need.

Given my path through life so far, I have learned that everything is vanity if not connected to Christ. All the striving, if not God centered, is a waste. I learned through experience that even being a world-known successful chef, I was not able to share Jesus with the people I was closest to because I wasn't doing things for the right reason. It's so important for us to be an example of the Lord, to make connections with others by reflecting the Lord's love and by being a bridge to help them meet the Lord. In other words, we need to glorify Him, not ourselves. The only way to do that is to keep Christ as the center. He's the only bridge builder between sinful man and our Holy God and taking that bridge enables us to rest in Him.

Key Scriptures

All of this leads me to a couple of my favorite scriptures, because they speak to my journey and provide me peace:

"Your word is a lamp to my feet, and a light for my path."

- PSALM 119:105

"I keep my eyes always on the Lord. With him at my right hand, I will not be shaken."

- PSALM 16:8

Duane Doyle

Listen and Converse

I was born into a Christian family. My parents and all four grandparents were born again believers in Jesus Christ as their Savior. My grandparents all came to the Lord in their 30's. My grandmother, Geraldine Doyle attended Neighborhood Church at the original Oakland location with my Dad and his younger brother and my namesake Duane.

Duane's tragic death in 1938 brought my grandpa Doyle to faith in Jesus. The church rallied around the young Doyle family in its most difficult trial and Pastor Earl Sexour said this was the catalyst for much growth at Neighborhood Church at that time.

My grandparents Peterson began attending the new church at 8411 MacArthur Blvd. in Oakland. Both of my grandfathers served on the board and as ushers for most of the rest of their lives. I remember sitting with them in their usher seats at the back of the center section on alternating Sundays. Doyle was on the left side and Peterson was on the right. We continued this practice at the new 3Crosses in Castro Valley. My grandparents were great examples to me of living Christian values and I observed my grandparents' devotion to reading God's word every day.

I accepted Jesus as my Lord and Savior at Neighborhood Church in Oakland on November 28th, 1963. Millie Story was the leader of "Children's Church" held in the Crimson Chapel and she prayed with me and several other kids that day to accept Jesus as Lord. Growing up in a Christian home and accepting the Lord at age seven does not make for a dramatic testimony but I am very blessed.

I have always wondered if pride would have been an obstacle at an older age, but my Lord spared me that challenge. I played saxophone in the Church Orchestra every Sunday night from 7th grade through college, attended camp every summer and attended mid-week advanced Bible studies taught by "Big Ed" Harris.

In college, Paul Travis challenged me and several of my friends to consider going into the ministry. I had spent much of my young life working as a mechanic at Peterson Tractor. I loved the heavy machinery and was focusing on a career at Peterson. The challenge from Paul really bothered me because of the conflict between my dreams and the possibility the Lord wanted me to go into ministry. I finally got to the point where I said, "Lord, if you want me in the ministry, I will do it." The Lord's answer came crystal clear. He said, "I just wanted you to be willing to do my will. You don't need to go into ministry." A huge burden was lifted from my soul by being willing to obey my Lord Jesus!

The example of daily Bible reading from my grandparents is a practice I cherish every day of my life. On some days, God's word speaks to me more than others, but I know that being consistent in reading, which I equate to "listening," and prayer, which I equate to "conversing," are the most essential components of my life.

I have been on the Neighborhood Church/3Crosses board for more than 30 years and appreciate the responsibility the Lord has entrusted to me. I would, however, consider leading a small group of men as my greatest joy in service to my Lord. Our group comes from all walks of life and several started as seekers but now have Jesus as their savior, too.

I am blessed with a wonderful, talented and patiently supporting wife of 44 years. I also have two believing children and their wonderful spouses and six super grandkids. I could go on and on about all of God's blessings, but the greatest is the blessed assurance of our salvation and Christ's coming victory over all.

Ed Hubbard

Maintain Proper Direction

My testimony begins before the earth was created, when God graciously chose me to be His object of saving love (Ephesians 1:4, John 15:16). Jesus lived my perfect life, obeying all of God's commands and resisting all temptation. He then absorbed God's fierce wrath against the sins of all Believers, died in my place, arose from the dead, and returned to Heaven, where He currently reigns (Psalm 97:1).

God regenerated me (John 1:12-13) as a child nearly 70 years ago, called me (Romans 8:30), justified me (Romans 8:30), redeemed me (Romans 3:24) and adopted me (Ephesians1:5). I realized that I was a sinner and alienated from God. A guest evangelist was speaking in our church when I felt the prompting of the Holy Spirit to ask my father for permission to get out of my seat and walk the long aisle to the platform to receive spiritual guidance. I remember the evangelist saying, "Here is the first child to come to the Lord this week." In the prayer room, I wept over my sins (Matthew 5:3), repented and believed in the Gospel (Mark 1:15).

My testimony continues today. I am on an adventure like no other — the adventure of sanctification: becoming what I am in Christ (Colossians 3:10). Continually changing. Continually conforming. Some days two steps forward and three steps backwards. Never perfection, but maintaining the direction. As C.S. Lewis said, "I know that I am made for another world because nothing in this world can ever satisfy my longings."

Something to Pass Along

Be 100% certain that you are a Believer. Know what you believe and why you believe it. How do I know that I am redeemed? The Book of 1 John gives several tests of the genuineness of our faith. The primary one is love (1 John 4:8). We know that God is love, but do I love God? Do I love God enough to regularly talk to Him in prayer? Do I love God enough to enjoy listening to Him by reading and studying His Word? Do I love God enough to want to please Him in all of my thoughts and actions? Do I love others? (1 John 4:20-21). Am I abiding in love (1 John 4:16)?

Know and embrace every attribute of God.

Know and embrace every precept and principle and promise found in God's Word.

Do not even try to synthesize scientism or the latest cultural "morality" with the Bible. View all of life through the lens of the Bible.

Do not add to or subtract from biblical truth. Do you want to hear God talking to you? Read the Bible. Do you want to hear God audibly talking to you? Read the Bible aloud.

Expect God to use you wherever you are and whatever you are doing in His name.

When I left my home and my home church to attend university, I knew I was saved and I believed the Bible, but my faith was sorely tested. I wish I had known then what I know now — but some things just take time.

Key Scripture

"Surely goodness and lovingkindness will follow me all the days of my life, And I will dwell in the house of the Lord forever."

- PSALM 23:6 NASB

Since "the days of my life" began at my conception, I have always enjoyed God's blessings and protection. Since "forever" means forever, I am saved forever which, of course, is the definition of eternal life.

Elaine Carvin

Keep Christ #1

I was born at 9:30am on May 25th. Yes, I kept my mother out of church that Sunday morning!

I was taken to Sunday school and taught about Jesus as a young child. One Sunday morning, the pastor gave an altar call and I went forward to dedicate my life to the Lord. Since then, I have had the most beautiful life following the Lord Jesus and asking Him to lead, guide and direct my life.

As the middle child of seven siblings, we were a very close-knit family. My mother played piano and we would all gather around her to sing beautiful hymns. Dad had a beautiful voice and could really sing the hymns! This is why I love 39ers class so much. I was raised on hymns and they are taken from the Scriptures.

All my life I have been guided by Jesus, the Scriptures and hymns. Every Sunday night at 9:00pm we would gather around the radio and listen to the preacher, his sermons, and his wife, Honey. She would read letters from the congregation that were beautiful and very blessed. At the same time every Sunday night in California, there was a young man named Duke who was listening to the same preacher. To this day I feel that the Lord planned for us to meet each other.

When I graduated from high school in 1947, my family and I left the farm and moved to California. My oldest brother was captain of the *President Johnson* Merchant Marine vessel and his first mate was the brother of the young man who had been listening to the Sunday night preacher. God planned my life, and my husband's, and we enjoyed 63 wonderful years together serving the Lord. He was raised at Melrose Baptist church in Oakland while I was raised at a Baptist church 30 miles north of Branson, Missouri. Can you believe it? We were 3,000 miles apart and God used my brother, The Sea Captain, and his brother, The First Mate, to introduce me to my husband, Duke Carvin.

This is my advice for the next generation: Young people, you must put Christ first in your life! Next, find a good Bible-teaching church and "Lean on the Lord and He will direct your life." He has given us so many promises, including, "I will never leave or forsake you." Read your Bible because it is your guide to living a life for Christ.

Key Scripture

"I have been crucified with Christ, and it is no longer I who live, but Christ lives in me; and the life which I now live in the flesh I live by faith in the Son of God, who loved me, and delivered Himself up for me."

- GALATIANS 2:20

My favorite hymn is: "What a day, Glorious day, When my

Jesus I shall See."

Christian fellowship is so important. We have had so many friends at 3Crosses who have gone on to be with the Lord but God said we will know each other and have a new spiritual body. I am looking forward to seeing Duke and my friends again. Thank you, Lord, for my 3Crosses church, Sunday School class, hymns, prayer-chain, Pastor Randy (my Sunday school teacher), the church board (godly people with wisdom), godly women for Women's Fellowship and Butch Monk and Eric Halverson (for our testimony request).

Eric Halverson

He Never Let Go

I was born in Toronto, Canada in 1952, but my parents moved to California when I was a baby and I was raised primarily in the San Francisco Bay Area. My parents were Christians and my brother and sister and I were brought up attending church. It was while living in San Lorenzo and attending San Lorenzo Community Church, however, that the family became very active in church. I attended Sunday school regularly, participated in the youth group and enjoyed a family life in which the church played a large role. In 1965, at the age of 13, I completed my "confirmation" classes and was accepted as a believing member of the United Church of Christ.

However, the following year my parents moved the family from San Lorenzo to Castro Valley and we effectively stopped attending church and the faith-based activities we had been involved in. I started attending Hayward High in 1966. The late 60's in the Bay Area was a challenging time for a high schooler, what with the Summer of Love, Woodstock, "Drugs, Sex, Rock n Roll," political assassinations, and the Viet Nam War. By my third year of high school, I had left my Christian faith and was a confirmed atheist, choosing science and intellect over religious superstition, as I viewed it. Although I was a good student, it wasn't long before my focus was on playing guitar, singing, chasing girls and partying. In other words, drinking, smoking and getting high.

Between 1968 and 1970, the war in Viet Nam had escalated to its greatest severity. Hundreds of thousands of young soldiers were being sent to fight overseas and tens of thousands of them were coming home dead, including two older high school friends of mine. The need for soldiers was so great that a non-volunteer draft lottery had been instituted (selection by birthdate) and young men were being drafted to fight in Viet Nam. The war that had once been popularly supported was now dividing the country. In my last year of high school, the draft was hanging over my head. I didn't want to think about it...but I knew it was coming.

I had entered high school in 1966 as a Christian believer and as a supporter of the military but by my graduation in June of 1970 I was a confirmed atheist and strongly anti-Viet Nam war. And now I was confronted with the draft. Shortly after my graduation, that year's lottery was held. My birthday was the 21st number drawn; I was going to be drafted and sent to Viet Nam.

But God, who had never let go of me, though I had let go of Him, began to slowly draw me back to Himself.

Because of the draft, I was now forced to think very seriously about the meaning of life, if it had meaning. Was I willing to go to war and kill? If not, why not? If Darwin was right, survival of the fittest was the rule for life. What value then was there in life? If it was OK to kill an animal in certain circumstances, wouldn't that same rule apply to man? Is man any different than the animals? Why? And if man is just another animal, and survival of the fittest (natural selection) is how the universe works, then killing not only should be OK, but expected. And what about morality? Natural Darwinism would reject the concept of any objective "morality" because everything is relative.

But I was conflicted. Being confronted with Viet Nam pitted what I had embraced intellectually (Darwinism, natural selection) against an internal witness that I had begun to recognize and just couldn't talk myself out of. Somehow, I knew that man was special, different than the animals. And somehow, I knew that there exists a universal morality that all cultures share and are obligated to. Murder is wrong, lying is wrong, oppressing the weak and helpless is wrong. Everywhere. All cultures. The answers provided by my secular humanism and Darwanism, the "intellectual scientific" theories and conclusions I had embraced, contradicted what I knew in my heart and in my soul. I knew that man was special. I knew that life mattered. I knew that universal morality was real. But why? I couldn't reconcile the contradiction between what my heart was telling me and what my mind was saying. I wrestled with this for weeks without understanding as I waited for my official draft notification.

Then one day, while meditating on these things and asking myself "What value is there in man that makes him special, above the animals?" I heard, not audibly, but somehow in my mind, somehow within my consciousness, "Because man is valuable to Me. I have assigned man a special place." Wait! What was happening? I had not reasoned this out and had not come up with this answer on my own. If I had, I would have heard, "Because man is valuable to God (3rd person)." But somehow, in a way I had never experienced before in my life, in a way difficult to explain, I heard "Because man is valuable to Me," in the first person!

I was dumbstruck! Did that really happen? But it was THE ANSWER I had been seeking; the only answer that made sense. God had given man his special place, his special significance over the rest of the animals. God had embedded within man an objective morality that was universal. God was the answer to the questions I was wrestling with. God! God reconciled the truth my heart insisted on with my mind's reason.

I now knew and believed...God was real! He was the Creator and He had created man as a special being for Himself. And dare I believe it? God had spoken to me!

And God, who had never let go of me, though I had let go of Him, continued to draw me back to Himself.

But now that I believed in God again, which God? My search was not over. I reasoned that there are many "gods" and many religions in the world. I needed to find the real one. But how?

I decided that I would not go to Viet Nam and kill, so I filed for "conscientious objector" status with my draft board and while awaiting their decision, enrolled at Chabot Junior College. As luck (?) would have it, there was a philosophy class on "World Religions" being offered, so I signed up for the class to continue my search for the "real" God.

The format of the class was that we would study each major religion by reading significant portions from each religion's "holy books." We read from the Koran (Islam), then the Bhagavad Gita (Hindu), and then Zen (Buddhist). Then we read the book of Genesis for the Jewish religion. Finally, we were assigned to read the Gospel of John for the Christian religion.

I was at home alone one rainy December morning, doing homework and preparing for my afternoon classes at Chabot. I picked up where I had been reading in John chapter 8. As I began to read, the words began to affect me in a way that none of the other religious readings had.

"I am the light of the world, he who follows me shall not walk in darkness, but have the light of life."

Reading the words began to have a physical affect on me. My stomach tightened and I began to tremble. I stopped reading, composed myself, laughed at myself for this weird reaction, and started reading again.

"If you knew me, you would know My Father also."

"He who sent me is true, and the things I heard from Him, these I speak to the world."

Again, I had to stop reading. Why was this book affecting me so? The other religious books had been easy to read. Now I was unable to get through more than a paragraph at a time without beginning to shake and without my eyes beginning to fill with tears.

"Truly, truly I say to you, everyone who commits sin is the slave of sin."

"If therefore the Son shall make you free, you shall be free indeed."

Reading was difficult but I had to finish the chapter before class so I continued to read.

"Your father Abraham rejoiced to see my day, and he saw it and was glad. The Jews therefore said to him, You are not yet fifty years old, and have you seen Abraham? Jesus said to them, "Truly, truly I say to you, before Abraham was born, I am."

When I read this it was as if I heard Jesus say "I AM" directly to me. The power of His words, "I AM," overwhelmed me. And I knew. I fell to my knees and wept. I knew then that Jesus was the Son of God and my search was over. I prayed simply "Jesus, I want to know you. Please forgive me. Please reveal yourself to me and lead me into Your truth."

And God, who had never let go of me, though I had let go of Him, in great patience and faithfulness, had brought me back to Himself.

And the draft? Miracle #1- the draft board approved my CO status, which almost never happens! Miracle #2- the draft board asked me if I preferred to have a student deferment instead so I could continue with my college studies. They had already announced publicly that they would not be giving out any more student deferments. So I continued my studies and began my Christian walk. The active draft was discontinued in 1973. I graduated in 1974 with a BA in Philosophy. The war in Viet Nam ended in 1975.

To the Next Generation

The Christian walk, our journey, the "race" as Paul framed it, is not a sprint. It is a long-distance marathon and that requires a different frame of mind. It requires endurance, steadfastness, patience and a lot of trust that the One who called us to start the race is also the One who is able to get us across the finish line. Realize that there will be both good and bad times; both easy and tough times. The tough times may be harder than you ever thought possible; illnesses, deaths, broken relationships, career setbacks are but a few of life's tragedies that befall believer and nonbeliever alike. There may be times when you hurt so bad you want to stop. But don't stop walking. Never give up. This too shall pass. Jesus will see you through. He who promised is He who is faithful and He will do it. He has given you His Spirit as a pledge, a guarantee. You are His, and He will not forsake you.

Key Scriptures

"The Lord will accomplish what concerns me; Thy lovingkindness, O Lord, is everlasting."

- PSALM 138:8

"If we confess our sins, He is faithful and just to forgive us our sins and to cleanse us from all unrighteousness.

- 1 JOHN 1:9

"There is therefore now no condemnation for those who are in Christ Jesus"

- ROMANS 8:1

The three scriptures quoted above are special to me because I am a sinner. When I first accepted Christ as my Lord, I gave in to sin regularly, but these scriptures convinced me not to give up. Forty-seven years later, the Spirit has thankfully worked in my life, but I am still just a forgiven sinner that finds comfort in these verses.

Fern Wallace

I'll Live On

When I was seven years old, we attended a family reunion on my mother's side in the state of Wisconsin. I was reared in a Christian home and attended Sunday School and children's church. I had heard about the way to heaven, but never made the decision to receive Christ into my heart.

One night I was overcome wlth a dreadful feeling of dying and going to hell. I wasn't ready for heaven! I wanted my mother to pray for me, but was prevented from waking her up by my cousin. She sat me up on the ironing board she was using and gave me a lemon to suck on. She said I could go quietly into the bedroom and check to see if my mother was awake. I knelt before her and listened to her breathing in and out and quite deep in sleep, so I was afraid to rouse her at all.

When I awakened the next morning that awful dread had passed so I never told my mother of the experience. I had not died and passed it off as a strange experience.

At the age of ten, I heard two visiting missionaries speak in church and they ended their time by singing "I'll Live On." I knew that I would not "live on" until I made things right with God. So I went forward to the altar, kneeling down to repent in tears, and receiving an overwhelming gift of peace. I wanted to share the good news of salvation and forgiveness with everyone. Of course, I shared that experience with my mother.

I like to say that sucking on a lemon will not take your sins away, but the precious blood of Jesus definitely will. All you have to do is ask.

Fred Porter

My Consolation

This story begins in Pontiac, Michigan. I was born in 1942 into a marriage that lasted about one and a half years following my birth. My biological father loved someone more than my mother so they were divorced in 1943. In the summer of 1944, when I was two, my mother and grandparents packed their belongings and moved to Los Angeles to avoid a custody suit brought by my father in Michigan. In those days he had no jurisdiction in California.

My mother and grandparents were Methodists, although they did not attend church on a regular basis, but they saw to it that I attended Sunday school at local churches or community centers whenever possible. I was taught many Bible stories and knew about God, but I did not know the God of the Bible. However, even then I felt God's hand on my life.

In 1949 my mother married a man who was attending the Los Angeles Police academy. During that first year he decided to leave the academy and join the Army to become a Military Police officer. Following the completion of his training in 1950, the Army stationed us in Oakland, California where we lived in the projects until 1954. Later that year we were assigned to Munich, Germany for one-year tour of duty where I attended a Sunday school on the Military Base.

In late 1955 we returned to the United States when my father was once again stationed in Oakland. Following our return my parents bought a home in San Lorenzo so that I could attend Arroyo High School and finally have permanent roots. All of this led me to a friendship that became my introduction to a life of faith.

My mother found a job working at a local bank with a woman whose son was also attending Arroyo High School and was in the same grade. She told me about this woman and her son and asked me to introduce myself to Steve and perhaps strike up a friendship. Little did I know that this was an appointment set up by the Lord.

Shortly after Steve and I became friends, he asked me if I wanted to attend a boy's club at his church in Oakland. They did crafts and other activities there, which sounded fun, so I accepted. That was my introduction to The Neighborhood Church. I enjoyed myself so much that I began attending the Junior High group on Sundays and eventually signed up for Junior High camp at Mt. Hermon the following summer. It was at that Junior High camp that I came to realize that God's grace pursued my heart and I committed my life to serving Him.

I became involved in (Omega) High School leadership, later in the college group, and finally, I became involved in adult ministries. In 1958 I met my future wife and we were married in 1964 by former pastor Dr. Jacob Bellig.

After High School, I decided I needed to extend my education so I enrolled at the College of San Mateo. After the first semester, I found that I wasn't ready for the college experience. I also realized that I was vulnerable for the draft. Many of the young men I knew were being drafted into the Army and, as an Army kid, I knew I didn't want to wind up in the regular Army. A friend at church suggested I consider the California National Guard where I could serve and still stay at home and work and accomplish my yet to be determined goals. So, I joined in 1961 and did my basic training and returned home to complete my obligation until my service was completed in 1969.

Following our marriage in 1964 we had three sons over the next 10 years. Our marriage lasted 49 years until her death in 2014. We raised our sons in the church and then, as it happens in many families, our sons were seduced by the music culture.

Early in 2003 we discovered our youngest son had become a heroin addict. He was arrested and placed in the court system where he was convicted of using illegal drugs and sentenced to six months in jail. With God's help and our love, he overcame his addiction. Today this amazing young man is an English Teacher teaching the English language to German students in Frankfurt, Germany.

Our middle son got his education in architecture and has become a successful designer and businessman here in the Bay Area. He has a beautiful family with three children and is giving them a multi-cultural education both here and in Mexico where they were born.

In early 2008 our oldest son quit the band life after having become a professional rock musician, and who for 15 years had toured both nationally and internationally with a major rock band. We saw that he was depressed and exhausted and needed help, so we volunteered our home to him at Lake Tahoe. I thought this would help him find himself and help restart his life. However, I didn't realize that this somehow only deepened his depression and sense of isolation.

I had started going to Lake Tahoe a couple times a month to spend time and attend church with him and I felt he was making progress. However, in June of 2010 while going to spend the weekend with him, we discovered he had committed suicide. Even today, I cannot reconcile his death because, as his father, it feels that I should have noticed the warning signs. But I believe God knew his heart and brought him home. (Isaiah 57:1-2) That alone is my consolation.

In 1975 I decided to start my own business as a Painting Contractor. I became successful and felt I could be equally successful as a builder so in 1982 I bought a large piece of property for a subdivision. I had to overcome many obstacles on the project, including a law suit over the fraudulent sale of the property. After more than a year I was not able to continue the suit and was forced to surrender the property and file for bankruptcy. This was a desperate time for our family as I had invested everything into this project. We eventually lost our home and savings and needed God's help. Almost immediately our real estate agent friend found us a rental home where we were able to live for the next 11 years.

For 10 years I struggled to get us back on our feet financially and continued to pray that God would provide relief from this struggle. In 1992 I was recruited by a friend to join the maintenance staff at Macy's department stores and was able to close down my contracting business and find financial security. During the following four years I was able to prove my skills and expertise to my superiors and was promoted to

Senior Executive of our division. This completely changed my trajectory and opened new doors. After 8 years I left my employment at Macy's and joined a project management company where I became a construction manager for Target Stores.

Looking back, I can clearly see God's hand in all of this. Although my eagerness put my family at risk, God was able to both teach me new skills and point me toward a career change that proved to be successful for our family. Never rule out God no matter how desperate you feel. He has a plan and you can trust Him to carry it out.

God also opened the door to ministry for me early in my life. In 1959 I joined the choir and the Sunday evening group called The Choralaires where I served for 18 years. God's hand was guiding me and opening doors for future ministry. During the years I served in The Choralaires, I became a member of a quartet which was very popular and performed regularly on Sunday nights during the musical portion of the Sunday evening program.

In 1975 our quartet performed at the Bay Area Sunday School Convention. We were the opening group for the main concert that evening, the Covenant Four Quartet who were based out of San Francisco. I remember meeting these men and hearing about their travels and ministry and wishing that I could join a professional ministry like theirs and use my musical talents on a broader scale.

Surprise! In 1978 the Lord answered the desire of my heart and I was contacted by a friend who was a composer and producer for the Covenant Four Quartet and he asked me to audition for them. Although I had been doing vocals for a local recording studio, my concern was that I might not be talented enough for such an amazing ministry. But the Lord knew what

He had invested in me and provided this opportunity. At the audition I was accepted and asked to join and for the next 35 years I sang with the Quartet. There was traveling, 15 recorded albums, radio and TV, and performing all over the western and central United States and Alaska. It was a wonderful period in my life and, as the word tells us, it was "beyond all that we desire or even think."

Up to this point I have described how I came to discover and accept God's work of grace and redemption in my life and the blessings I have experienced through that grace. But my life has had its tragedy and pain. God has not promised us an easy life. In fact, most of us who reach our age have discovered that life can be very difficult. But God has promised to be with us and be our delight (Prov. 3:5-6).

Following my wife's death in 2014, my sons were concerned about my state of mind and suggested I call on one of our friends with whom we had been close for more than 40 years. She was widowed after losing her husband a decade before and my wife and I had stayed close to her through the following years. My sons saw that I needed companionship beyond what they could provide. Here again, God had a plan for my future. So, I called her and suggested we have lunch as friends. That friendship continued and grew into a love that brought us both together to form the miraculous marriage we have today. Pat is the miracle of my life and I wake up every morning and thank God for her love, grace, and beautiful spirit. God completes our lives through his wonderful gifts. We have been married for four and a half years and counting and every new day in a miracle.

In my life I've suffered business failures and successes and many things have interacted at any one time. I've lost a child and family members and through all of this He has loved me and been my comfort. As I look back over my 78 years, I can see His hand in all of it. God knows our hearts and the Psalms tell us that he planned every day of our lives before we were born. He knows the hardships and victories and provides His love and care through it all. The one consistent in my life has been the hand of God. I have lived a full life and a rich life and with whatever days remain, I will serve him until the end.

In conclusion, no matter where you are in your life, no matter your age or financial situation or other hardships, God knows all of it and has a plan to see you through to eternity. God uses everything in our lives to bring glory to himself. All he needs is our trust and faithfulness. Stay close to Him and trust in Him and He will be your delight.

Key Scriptures

*"Trust in the Lord with all your heart and lean not on your own understanding; in all your ways submit to him, and he will make your paths straight." *

- PROVERBS 3:5-6

"The righteous perish, and no one ponders it in his heart; devout men are taken away, and no one understands that the righteous are taken away to be spared from evil. Those who walk uprightly enter into peace; they find rest as they lie in death."

- ISAIAH 57:1-2

Helene Granath

God is in Control

How I became a Christian: I saw the change in a person's life when I was 22 years old and I knew I wanted that in my life also. I was raised Catholic so I had some understanding of God but I did not have a personal relationship with Him. I did not know you needed to invite Jesus into your life in order to become a child of God. So when I found out that is what was needed, I did it. Psalm 40:3b says, "Many will see and fear and put their trust in the Lord."

Key Scripture

I love reading 2 Chronicles 20:6-12, which says, "O Lord God of our fathers, are you not the God who is in heaven? (v. 7) O our God, did you not ... (v12) O our God, will you not...for we have no power to face this vast army that is attacking us. We do not know what to do, but our eyes are upon you."

It's a great reminder that God is the creator of the universe (v6) and that He is in control (v7). God will help you as he has done in the past (v12). God is there for your needs in the "here and now." There are insurmountable problems we all face and we don't know what to do, but if you lay the problems on Jesus, He will guide you.

What is a scripture that has special meaning for you? One of my favorite scriptures is Psalm 103:1-6. "Bless the Lord, O my soul and all that is within me, bless His holy name. Bless the Lord, O my soul, and forget not all His benefits. Who forgives all thine iniquities, who heals all thy diseases, Who redeems my life from destruction, Who crowns thee with lovingkindness and tender mercies, Who satisfies thy mouth with good things, so that thy youth is renewed like eagles. The Lord executes righteousness and judgment for all that are oppressed."

The reason I chose this is because it tells us how to be saved and the benefits. You go to the Lord (v2); Your sins need to be forgiven and you are healed spiritually as well as sometimes physically (v3); You were headed to hell before and now you have been given access to heaven and God's lovingkindness and mercy while here on earth (v4); The Lord satisfies your daily needs and gives you strength for daily activity (v5); We are declared righteous in God's sight through the blood of Jesus (v6); It goes from the moment you are saved till you go to the grave.

God is with you.

Jean Morrow

Yield Yourself to God

God has been incredibly good to me. It all began on July 26, 1939, when He brought me into an amazing Christian family. My dad, Howard Critchfield, had been an Assembly of God (AG) traveling evangelist who had to find work during the depression years to provide for his family of four. He took a job teaching at Monte Vista Christian School in Watsonville while my mom, Laura, stayed home with my older sister, Anita, and me.

When World War II broke out everyone plunged into war work. We moved to the Bay Area so Dad could go to work at the Kaiser Shipyards in Richmond, to build Victory Ships. We landed at his friend Irving Ford's place in Oakland, where Dad helped milk the cow and assisted in Reverend Ford's church.

In 1947 my parents decided to check out the new church they had watched being built on MacArthur Boulevard in Oakland: the Oakland Neighborhood Church. To Dad's delight, his old AG friend, David Von Rotz, was playing the organ. While we had always attended Assembly of God churches, Dad commented "If it is good enough for Dave, it is good enough for me!" We made the move to Neighborhood, primarily for the excellent youth programming.

I recall the powerful pull of the Holy Spirit on my young, pre-teen life. In the late 1940's we attended the evangelist faith-healing tent meetings of Oral Roberts in Alameda, where I went to the prayer tent and prayed to receive Christ. Then when Jacob Bellig became pastor in 1954, I went to the prayer room and counseled with Charlotte Bellig and made a more mature reconfirmation of my faith. Charlotte told me to read the New Testament each day, which I began doing. I was off to a good start!

When I was in high school the church began the annual fall Kick-Off Rallies at the beginning of football season. They were a very popular event and drew big crowds among high schoolers. I was very active in the Omega ministry at that time, serving as president during my senior year. I played in the orchestra and then sang in the Choralaires. The church was my life!

In 1957 I moved to Berkeley to start college at the University of California. I would say that the devil works overtime on college kids today, trying to derail their faith. It was my goal to be a missionary, a Wycliffe Bible Translator. Neighborhood Church sent me to Mexico during the summer between my sophomore and junior years to stay with a Wycliffe family, learn about missionary life, and bring back a report. I was excited and switched my college focus from a psychology major to linguistics.

But things got "fuzzy" for my faith and future as I mentally wrestled with the teachings of my atheistic professors, especially in psychology and anthropology. I began questioning my faith. I thought unbelievers "had more fun." I wanted in on that fun, and I made some really bad choices. I had a boyfriend and missionary work just wasn't going to blend in with what I wanted for my life. I wanted to marry Ray and stay home. He lived a very exciting life of symphonies, operas and world travel. While he was a Christian, there was no missionary future for him. Somehow, I ended up throwing out my faith and my missionary ambition to marry Ray.

While I gave up on God for a while, He never gave up on me. Oh, I continued to attend church; Ray saw to that. But I was confused and skeptical. I considered myself to be an "intellectual agnostic." In fact, I had chosen to disbelieve because it was convenient. I had been tricked and duped by Satan.

Ray took a job in Colombia, South America in 1969, and we lived there for two years. While there I completed my Ph.D. thesis, writing a grammar of the Car Nicobarese language. That language is spoken on the island of Car Nicobar, which is annexed to India. I had visited India twice to do research, and while I was there, I had the amazing privilege of a personal sit-down meeting with Jawaharlal Nehru, the Prime Minister of India.

Upon our return to California, we moved in with Ray's parents. While it was home to Ray, it was suffocating to me! To get out, I quickly got a real estate license and went to work in my dad's (then vacant) real estate office in Castro Valley. I loved selling real estate; it was so practical and down to earth, not acerbic and aimless as I considered college teaching to be. I had taught briefly, even having California governor Jerry Brown as one of my students!

Early in my sales experience a woman from Neighborhood Church named Elaine contacted me about relocating. Elaine and her husband had four children (I had none and that was just fine) and she had a very visible faith in God. She prayed about everything. At that point, I had a gnawing emptiness in my soul and a longing for something more. I had turned away from God. Ray and I had traveled until I was tired and I could have anything I wanted, but nothing could satisfy me.

Elaine was such a contrast. She hadn't been anywhere and had to struggle to figure out how they would buy the house, but she exuded contentment and joy. I wanted what she had! On inquiry, I learned that she attended a weekly Bible study which she said was just wonderful and gave her strength. She offered to pick me up and take me. I asked her where it was and told her I would be there at the very next meeting!

I will never forget that day, April 23, 1972. When I arrived late, as was my style—there were probably 300 women on their feet singing joyously. My heart surged with the feeling that I was coming home, that this was what was missing in my life and here I would get back on track with God. And I was right. I was assigned to a small group led by Jonette Richardson. Their group was having a luncheon after class in the home of one of the women and they urged me to attend.

After the small group meeting, everyone reassembled in the main hall of First Presbyterian Hayward and, after singing a song, we listened to a forty minute lecture explaining the lesson the ladies had just discussed in the small group. After the lecture I found the house where the luncheon was being held and enjoyed a kind of fellowship that I had never known. It was simply wonderful and that day my faith was reaffirmed.

One of the things the lecturer, Sandy Blackmun, said was, "If anyone wills to do His will, he shall know concerning the doctrine, whether it is from God or whether I speak on My own authority." That was from John 7:17. Hearing this verse made me realize that my lack of faith was not resultant from lack of evidence. It was due to a lack of will on my part to obey. I realized it was also due to my pride and willfulness, a desire to be my own master and not be answerable to anyone. I had determined that God was not knowable because He could not be found through the scientific method, and I considered myself to be a scientist. But when I humbled myself and said "yes" to God, that I would obey Him, He revealed to me that He was much greater than my mere, finite mind could dissect and analyze and "find."

Jeremiah 29:14 says, He will be found by those who seek Him in truth with a humble, willing heart. To those, He will reveal Himself. He revealed Himself to me. Salvation is a gift and even the ability to find God is a gift from Him. I am forever grateful for His grace to me.

God put a song in my heart that day and He definitely "Keeps Me Singing." Since then, life has been good: walking with Jesus every day, reading His Word, fellowshipping with His people. I can't imagine a better life than I have had. And I owe it all to Him.

Since coming back into fellowship with Jesus, it has been my desire to get the word out about His great salvation. Through the years God has given me many wonderful opportunities to serve Him, among them:

- Calling on visitors to the church to make them welcome
- Beginning and coordinating a bus ministry for Sunday School
- Inviting people door-to-door in Castro Valley to attend the church
- Playing trumpet in the church orchestra

- Leading small group Bible studies for more than forty years
- Beginning and coordinating a guest reception ministry on Sundays
- Serving as Bay Area Women's coordinator for the 1996 Billy Graham Crusade
- Joining and serving with the Auxiliary of the Gideons International, which continues to be a wonderful motivator and enabler to sharing my faith
- Working as an online missionary with Global Media Outreach, through which I have worked with 672 people throughout the world to date

To those who know Christ, I would say God has not called us to sit and stew. We are to "occupy until He comes," as it says in Luke 19:13. We are never too old to serve the Lord.

To those who think they "don't need God," I would say I found it was possible to have a fairly good life apart from God. But when I allowed Christ into my life, I became dramatically more contented and full of joy. The emptiness was gone. On top of that, I have assurance of eternal life. This is life at its best!

To those who say they can't find God or don't know if there is a God, I would say "Yield!" Humble yourself and yield as much of yourself to God as you can understand. Ask Him to reveal Himself to you, and tell Him, and yourself, you will believe and obey Him when He does. And He will reveal Himself to you.

To everyone, I would say God is good! He is "what" makes life worth living. Take Him as your own Lord and Savior!

Jeni Lambel

How About Now?

I have been a believer nearly all my life but back in 2005 something went wrong. My husband of 30 years passed away to be with our Lord. I had already experienced the pain of my dear father's passing a year earlier. I was not prepared for either of the two most important men in my life to join our Lord.

A friend suggested a glass of wine would help me sleep. Long story short...one glass turned into a bottle, then a box. Over the next ten years, I found myself drunk 3-4 nights out of every week. I kept a good job but many mornings I went to work hung over, or at least a little buzzed.

Time after time I prayed to my God to help me stop drinking. I thought He wasn't listening. I remained a "good Christian" and attended church and prayed every night for His help. It didn't come.

A doctor I was seeing asked on many occasions, "when do you think you will stop drinking?" or "don't you think it is time to stop drinking?" Well, this just went in one ear and out the other for years. Until one day he asked his usual question and it was the "last straw." I said to him, "sure, how about now?" He picked up a phone and called Kaiser Hospital's Chemical Dependence Recovery Program. At the same time, I was advised (required) to join Alcoholics Anonymous.

In AA they asked me to "get" a Higher Power. Well, I already had my Lord, and He wasn't doing much to help me. But I played along with the commitment I had made to my doctor and myself. Week after week went by and I had stopped drinking. Weeks turned into months and months into years. Today I can say that I have been clean and sober for five years and counting.

Sometime in the last five years, I realized God wasn't ignoring my pleas. He was waiting for me to work with Him and not to expect Him to work a miracle and take this ailment from me.

He was with me the entire time. He just knew it had to be my decision to help myself. My requests, although I thought sincere, were really empty. When I decided to work with God, He helped me.

How many times throughout my Christian life have I asked God for something, sat back, and expected Him to take care of it?

Now I understand what it means, "with God's help I can do almost anything."

Josephine Wong

Go Tell the World

I grew up in an atheistic home. But my father, an Asian American soldier who fought in Europe during WWII, encouraged us four kids to attend church to become "good." On Easter 1966 I chose to follow our Lord, who found me and loved me first. Here is what I recall how my salvation came to be:

I had a high school classmate (whom I will call "Hannah" here) who one day said something odd sounding to me. In discussing our upcoming Latin exam, Hannah said, "I believe in prayer."

Instead of writing her off, I listened. I was curious why Hannah would believe in an invisible God. Hannah invited me to her Friday night college/high school fellowship, "Souls for Christ Fellowship (SFC)" in Oakland. I accepted her invitation as a way for me to have something to do on Friday nights. There was laughter, Singspiration, creative skits, Bible Study and sincere sounding prayer. It was my first exposure to young believers and I wondered why they seemed so happy and sincere in their faith. I listened and observed and attended for months.

Then I got scared and quit going to Friday nights. I knew that I wasn't one of them, which troubled me.

But Hannah remained my friend and invited me to join her at a 3-day Spring retreat at Redwood Alliance woods. Through the gift of a church scholarship, I went, but by the second evening, I had decided not to participate in that night's campfire. I still could not "see" and understand God like them. This troubled me.

I skipped dinner that evening and while trying to fall asleep in my lonely bungalow, I found myself asking God to show Himself. With a sad heart, I fell asleep in the darkness and stillness of the bungalow.

The next thing that happened is hard for me to explain. The bungalow light suddenly flashed, awakening me from my slumber. Girls were returning from the campfire and one of them threw herself on her bed, sobbing and crying out, "I'm no good. No good! I failed Him." Other girls surrounded her with words of comfort.

What she blurted out and her grief over being “useless,” allowed my heart to finally understand that there was a Loving Father God who loved me for being "NO GOOD. NO GOOD!" I can't explain it but on that Easter 1966, I became an authentic Christ-follower. I became born-again (John 1:12). I loved Him then, I love Him now, and His Word is precious to me. For, once I was blind, but now I see.

By God's grace, I have served our Lord in many different ways as He's provided me service opportunities. My heart is to "GO! GO! GO and tell others!" I've been told that I'm evangelistic. I can't help myself! I've had opportunities to serve in various capacities in the church, including as a facilitator for 17 years in BSF and recently in GriefShare. I am called now to pray for my children and grandchildren, for my family members, for my neighborhood and for missionaries who serve sacrificially. Presently I'm called to serve my husband who is learning to manage his partial blindness with the help of the Society for the Blind.

He has granted me a loving family, with my children also following our Lord. My parents, my brothers and many of my friends have become Christians because God has emboldened me then and now to share how REAL He is. By His Spirit, I live on this side of the River telling others of Him being real. I look forward to being in the Presence of Our Heavenly King. For those who have gone before me and now enjoy His presence, I just think, "What a wonderful reunion that will be!"

Key Scripture

Galatians 5:16 says, "So I say, live by the Holy Spirit's power. Then you will not do what your sinful nature wants you to do."

Galatians 4 speaks of the struggle Paul saw between those of the law and those of Spirit. Just as twins Esau (flesh) and Jacob (God's promise) struggled in the womb, I struggle in my weakness yet in Christ.

"I can do all things through Him who strengthens me."

(PHILIPPIANS 4:13)

Dear Heavenly Father

Thank You for Paul's warning not to be swayed by the flesh and remain with old comfortable habits. Thank You that even though Paul could have thrown in the towel, he kept on course and completed his race. Thank You that I understand You in Your Word now.

Thank You that I can hope in the reality of a Kingdom that I will soon become a part of. Help me to not throw in the towel. Help me to stay the course. Help me to complete the race that You set before me. Help me to rely on Christ alone to guide my thoughts. Give me Your Peace! I boldly ask in Jesus' Precious and Holy Name. Amen.

Larry Vold

Be Known for Your Love

My parents introduced me to Jesus through the way they lived and by bringing me to church with them when I was a child. The Lord spoke into my heart as I memo-rized Scripture as a child while attending Vacation Bible School at the Baptist Church my family attended. Scripture memorization laid the foundation for that special moment when Jesus came knocking at my heart's door as an elementary-aged child and I opened it, asking Him to come in. Throughout the years that followed, (and even those that preceded) I sincerely believed God loved me and wanted to lead me. Opening my life to Jesus in 3rd grade, however, brought about an even greater confidence of this.

My life as a child of God wasn't stretched or challenged in any significant way until I reached high school. It was there when I began recognizing the difference between those who really knew and followed Jesus and those who didn't. During my freshman year, I took a passive posture toward following

Jesus, which began to erode some of my convictions about my faith, leaving me to appear much like any of my friends, even those who didn't know or walk with God. While I didn't see what was happening to me, my faith was truly being tested and I wasn't passing the test.

Thankfully, at the end of my sophomore year, the Baptist church where I had received Jesus' gift of salvation, hired a youth pastor to focus on the spiritual formation of the teens who attended there. This youth pastor's personal concern for my life and example as a believer turned my life around. I realized I could no longer straddle the fence and be passive in my walk with Jesus. I realized that to follow Jesus meant denying myself and picking up my cross daily to follow Him (Luke 9:23). During the middle of my first high school summer camp, I went forward in a meeting at the invitation of the speaker, to fully give my life over to Jesus and His plans for me.

This was a significant turning point in my life. I suddenly found myself concerned for the spiritual well-being of others. I wanted others to know Jesus like I knew him. I wanted the joy and love I felt deep inside to be shared with anyone I met. I became somewhat of an evangelist on my high school campus. Many of my classmates were introduced to Jesus through my testimony and also through inviting them to attend my church youth ministry. The Lord did something very special in those years as hundreds of high school students from four high school campuses near my church became Christ-followers. I witnessed the power of the gospel and the way God loves to use anyone who is willing to be used for His work!

After high school, my goal was to become a career firefighter. I felt that by having this kind of vocation, I could remain busy as a volunteer in my local church and also do something very exciting with my life. But God had other plans. As I was finishing up my fire science courses at a local junior college and pursuing various fire departments for interviews and testing, a young high school student began attending our youth ministry. This young man was deeply entrenched in the occult and was manifesting characteristics that showed me the reality of the spiritual dimension in Ephesians 6:12. "Our struggle is not against flesh and blood, but against rulers, against the authorities, against the powers of this dark world and against the spiritual forces of evil in the heavenly realms."

Watching God's work in delivering this young man from his bondage to sin and the devil through the gospel, made me yearn to be more involved in seeing others find freedom through Jesus Christ. God used this season in my life to call me into vocational ministry. Soon after receiving this call, I enrolled in a Christian liberal arts college and got my degree in Christian education while serving as a part time youth leader in the church's youth ministry I had attended from childhood.

After graduating from college, I was hired by a local church in San Jose and began my work as a full-time youth pastor. This was an amazing time in my life, but the church went through some struggles which eventually resulted in them letting me go. But God used this to strengthen my trust so that I could trust what the future held for me. Eventually, I was led to serve as a youth pastor at The Neighborhood Church in Castro Valley (now known as 3Crosses) where I've been ever since.

I met my wife at 3Crosses through a student-ministry event that solicited the help of adults. She was one who came to volunteer and it wasn't long before I fell deeply in love with her. We married in 1982 and, in time, God blessed us with three children—all girls! We all enjoyed an amazing season of life with my serving in various positions in the church before eventually becoming the senior pastor in 1996.

In 2019, I stepped away from my role as senior pastor and yet continue to serve in our church as pastor of spiritual care. I will never stop thanking God for his faithfulness in allowing me to serve as a pastor in various roles for all these years in such an amazing Gospel-centered Church! He's been so faithful and generous for giving me a beautiful wife and loving children who are now adults. My wife and I celebrate 39 years of marriage this year and the joy of three beautiful grandsons (and maybe more some day!) Life isn't easy or perfect, but God is working out everything for my good and His glory (Romans 8:28).

Now that I'm in my 60s and recognize that it won't be too long before I leave this world to enter the glories of my heavenly home (which I also realize could be at any moment—God knows the number of our days as Psalm 139 reminds us), I think of a few things I wish to convey to the younger generation. First, I would remind them to value and leverage their youthfulness to the glory of God. I didn't, and most young people don't realize the blessing of being young! Ecclesiastes 12:1 states, "Remember your Creator in the days of your youth, before the days of trouble come and the years approach when you will say, 'I find no pleasure in them.'"

To be young is a gift for so many reasons. Youthfulness allows an almost limitless supply of energy. So much can be done because young people have so much energy! If that energy can be directed toward gospel-centered endeavors, so much good could come to our world! Be thankful for being young and use your youthfulness to bless others with the gospel of Jesus Christ!

The second thing would be to hold on to the truth of God's Word no matter what the cost. And the cost for doing this will be great, indeed. We are living in times when God's Word is under attack as never before. Even so-called pastors and churches have jettisoned the precious Word of God and chosen any number of sources to direct their lives and ministries apart from it.

The prophet Amos spoke of a time when there would be a famine for "hearing the words of the LORD" (Amos 8:11). Amos' prophetic warning applies to us today more than ever. There's a famine of God's Word everywhere today. It's hard to find churches that, without apology, teach that God's Word is the trustworthy source of divine revelation which must be the rule of our faith and practice. And of course, it's even more rare to find individuals today who hold with strong conviction that the Bible is God's unalterable Word!

Lastly, I would encourage both young and old to love God with all their heart and love others as they love themselves. Let love be what we're known for so that we can be used to share the message of hope found in Jesus Christ everywhere we go.

Lidia Furelos

Work Together in Peace

I was born in a Christian home in Córdoba, Argentina. What a blessing! My parents, Modesto and Constancia Zalazar, taught me about Jesus and dedicated their life to serve our Lord and Savior. Every day we had Bible Devotional, where we read and memorize verses of the Bible, and sang praises to the Lord. They always had one room in our home to worship the Lord and to praise His name. We used to go house by house inviting people to the service.

They preached and explained the love of God. Sometimes, we gathered together on the street corner, singing and telling others about Jesus. Papá always has the promise of Isaiah 55:11, "So is my word that goes out from my mouth; It will not return to me empty, but will accomplish what I desire and achieve the purpose for which I sent it."

In our neighborhood, there were families whose children did not read or write. Their parents asked our parents if it would be possible for me to teach their children. It was a very unique experience. In the Summer, Mamá would prepare lemonade with cookies and in Winter hot chocolate with homemade bread and cookies. The children were so happy and I was, too. There were times when we took the children to the Barrio Square, taught them the word of God, sang praises and learned a Bible verse and everybody left singing what they learned. What a joy that I will never forget!

The time came when Papá began visiting some big and small cities in different parts of Argentina, Bolivia and Chile. The Lord was helping him take the word of God to so many people. Mamá went with him on the train or bus sometimes while my older sister and brothers took care of us.

There was a marvelous time when the Lord provided a Bible coach (automobile). Papá and some brothers repaired it and filled the coach with Bibles, New Testaments, Christian magazines and clothes for so many people in need. They all were so happy and grateful and later many of them attended the services. It was great to see the Lord's help in action.

In 1968, I came to the United States and attended the 1st Baptist Church in San Francisco. The choir director invited me to go to the choir practice, which was just wonderful. To me it was like a dream. They all were so nice and friendly. I started learning English at the International Institute in San Francisco.

I met my husband, Jorge, in the Spanish Church in San Francisco and in July 1970 we got married. My brother lived in San Leandro. As my parents were planning to visit us, we all prayed, asking the Lord for a house to buy. Everything went quite smoothly and we bought our home; it was like a dream coming true. We enjoyed their company so much and took them to 3Crosses in Castro Valley. They saw such a big building and loved the three crosses in front of the church and the people who were so friendly and singing praises to the Lord. Other Sundays we took them to different Spanish Churches in the Bay Area as well. They preached and spoke to the congregation about their experiences. They really felt welcomed, happy and blessed.

I went to school in San Leandro and really wanted to learn about the USA; it was my dream to become a U.S. citizen. One of the Spanish teachers asked me if I could teach one of his classes about Argentina and also to teach them Spanish, show pictures and make the class attractive and interesting. My husband helped me to prepare all the material needed and we accomplished our purpose. We were very happy and grateful to the Lord. When I finished the courses in San Leandro High, I decided to go to Chabot College.

When I began looking for a job I went to different places, among them a bank in San Leandro where the manager and his assistant were very helpful. They gave me different tests and thank God I was feeling His company and His peace. When I finished and gave my tests to the manager, he asked me when I could start working and I said Now! The next week I was able to start working. They needed Spanish speakers and I loved to help in whatever ways necessary. I went to training and that was my entry into the bank where I worked for more than 28 years.

I started as a teller but moved on to Customer Service, New Accounts and eventually that invited me to work in Investments. The training was great and overall I enjoyed my job. If my customer was bringing a problem, my goal was to see him leaving with a smile.

I had the blessing to win some beautiful and challenging awards. I had the opportunity to go to Cancún and visit beautiful places, with excursions and surprises around every corner. I also visited New Orleans, San Francisco and Monterey and had many other excursions to different places. I also had the opportunity to meet employees from different branches who came to enjoy their awards. In all circumstances, Jorge was there with us and that made a big difference.

While I was working so hard at the bank I attended Chabot College where I was able to earn my Associate of Arts and Associate in Arts in Human Services degrees.

I had the promise from my Lord in Isaiah 58:9, "Then you will call, and the Lord will answer; you will cry for help, and he will say: Here am I."

As we were attending our church in Castro Valley, Pastor Leonetti from 1st Baptist Church in Union City asked us if we could help in his church. He needed to go to Argentina with his family. Well, that was a time to be praying and asking direction from the Lord. Yes, they left and we helped as much as we could. I was helping with the worship music, the Sunday school class for teen age girls, and serving the Lord wherever help was needed. It was a real blessing serving the Lord with my brothers and sister.

The pastor returned and we noticed the church was getting more crowded. We started working together, baking cookies and cakes and selling to the members. They all loved it and began making plans for how to enlarge the place. We had the land, so the brothers got permission from the city and we all started working and cooperating in the best way. We decided to host Flea Markets on Saturdays. The expansion took months of dedication but the brothers and sisters were ready to cooperate and sang, "If we all work together and in peace... what a joy that will be."

The Lord helped us from the beginning to the end. Many brothers had ideas for how to do the construction. They were all were doing different jobs but while serving the Lord. The day came when we finished our beautiful building; we all did our best to finish for the Lord. "Count your blessings, name them one by one, count your blessings see what God had done..."

Key Scripture

"Give thanks to the Lord Almighty, for the Lord is good. His love endures forever."

- JEREMIAH 33:11

Linda Decker

Step Out in Faith

I was raised in Oakland, California by parents who were believers, but they only attended church on Easter Sunday. I became a believer at the age of 12 and walked myself to church every Sunday. This was my early habit of worship that carried through junior and senior high school. After graduation from high school I went to work for Western Electric.

At the ripe old age of 18, I was married to Roger, my husband now of almost 60 years. We had two children, Dawn Ann and Keith Dwight. As they became older I sent them to Neighborhood Church on the bus that came to our Hayward neighborhood. The pastor then was Jacop Bellig. I also attended Challengers class in what is now called the Child Ministry Center. As the children got older we began weekend family camping trips, water skiing and fishing trips so church got put aside for quite a while. Once the kids were out of the house and on their own, I started going again, but not on a regular basis.

About 27 years ago I started attending Neighborhood Church again and after a couple of years suggested to my husband that he join me. He agreed and we have been members since 1996; we were both baptized on August 20, 2000. As members, we found our calling as ushers for the third service and we love all the fellowship involved with that position.

Key Scripture

My favorite bible verse is Psalm 23: 1-6, because it is what I feel in my heart about our Lord.

I would like to encourage all believers to step out in faith and get involved in activity within the church, because the more you do the more reward you receive.

Lucy Bauman

He Keeps Me Singing

I am 91 years old. It seems that I have been a Christian all my life, having been born into a Bible-believing family. But it wasn't until I was 16 years old and a freshman in college that I made a declaration to follow Jesus.

I have been going to Neighborhood Church/3Crosses for about 67 years. Walking with Jesus means that you are never alone. He is always there for you. All you have to do is reach out for Him.

Key Scriptures

Some of my favorite Bible verses are John 3:16 and Romans 8:35-39. I do not write them out as I want you to look them up and read them. These scriptures have given me a lot of comfort.

My advice to anyone is to get involved in your church, get into a Bible study, and read your Bible every day. You need this as much as you need your daily food.

Sometimes when I have a bad day, as everyone does, I sing this little song:

"Jesus, Jesus, Jesus, Sweetest name I know. Fills my every longing, keeps me singing as I go!"

Lynn Halverson

The Lord's Prayer

I was raised in a little town of 5,000 people. Cloverdale was parochial in many senses, a strong Catholic and Italian majority, and a couple of Protestant churches. Neighborhood Church was one of these. Yes, just like here. Pastor Larry Vold told me he knew some of the people from that congregation. I was not raised in either denomination. We celebrated the Christmas tree and the Easter basket but had no real connection to the meaning.

As a child, I was not happy at home for many of the social reasons that still plague the present day. I coped by being athletic, maintaining good grades and spending a lot of time at my friends' houses. I was blessed in many ways as I had a horse my entire childhood, a pool in my backyard and great teachers who provided me with a solid education.

I worked at a drug store, convalescent hospital and an open-air hamburger stand in my teens. One day at that hamburger stand an itinerant youth pastor invited me to a youth event at Neighborhood Church. Truth be told, if he wasn't as cute as he was, I wouldn't have gone. That evening, after all the kids had been hanging out, there was an altar call in the tiny chapel. I looked up at the cross and saw God patting his lap and saying," Come here, I'll be your dad." I ran forward and accepted Jesus into my heart! It was the best day of my life. He has guided me through many years of acceptance of His love and forgiveness towards others.

In my adult life, I have encountered many of the social issues my family was challenged with and have been taught great mercy and forgiveness that I am so grateful to have learned. Without Him, I know I would not have. Thank you Jesus, everyday!

Key Scripture

If I were to say something of use to a younger generation, I think I would focus on the Lord's Prayer. Always, always go there if you need His presence but don't know what to say or to ask for.

If you're facing past or present pain or just looking for the best way to start your day, always go there. His presence and the Holy Spirit's presence will arrive as you say or sing these words:

"Our father, who art in Heaven, hallowed be Thy name Thy Kingdom come, Thy will be done on earth as it is in Heaven.

Give us this day our daily bread and forgive us our trespasses

as we forgive those who trespass against us

and lead us not into temptation, but deliver us from evil.
For thine is the Kingdom, and the Power and the Glory forever and ever. Amen."

MATTHEW 6:9-13

Marjorie Johnson

The 4 Spiritual Laws

Until the age of eight, I lived on a peach ranch with my parents. I was the oldest of three girls, very happy and secure in my role at home and at school, liked and accepted by all of my classmates.

But suddenly we were forced to move from the ranch to Modesto because of a dispute between my father and his dad, who owned the ranch. The bottom fell out of my world. I changed from being self- confident to very shy and insecure, not knowing my new classmates and not feeling accepted by them.

As I look back on that time now, though, I can see the Lord's hand in this. Now that we lived in town instead of in the country, my sisters and I were able to freely attend church, not dependent on being driven into town. We would walk, roller skate or ride our bikes on Sunday mornings, while our mom stayed home on her only day off to do the laundry and the inevitable ironing.

I have such treasured memories of accepting Christ at an altar call at the age of eleven. My younger sister, Sharon, and I went forward, faced the congregation, and repeated the words after the pastor, accepting Jesus as our personal Savior.

My salvation experience was glorious and I wanted to sing praises and write poetry expressing my love for Jesus. But due to tension in the family over my dad's alcoholism, my insecurities never diminished.

At the age of 15, I became involved in a relationship with my future husband, Harold. Hal was very controlling, which contributed to us getting married when I was only 16, between my Junior and Senior years of High School. I did graduate from high school in 1955, while my husband was sent by the Marine Corps to Japan.

After graduation, I joined Hal as a military wife on his various assignments. I was able to join him when he was shipped off to Italy for three years. The experience of living abroad added an extra dimension to our lives. In 1963, we returned Stateside with 4-month-old baby Eric and a 1959 Maserati 3500 GT Coup. The Maserati had significance because it opened the door to what would become the primary source of income and focus for our growing family.

In 1965 our daughter Liz was born in Modesto. Then in 1968 Hal and I established our foreign car repair business in San Leandro, which still exists to this day, owned and operated by Eric. Our son Christopher (CJ) was born in Hayward in 1968.

One of our family's greatest difficulties stemmed from Hal's exces-sive drinking. He was also fiercely jealous of anything or anyone who would possibly take my time and attention away from him. He especially had a great hostility toward my relationship with the Lord and wouldn't allow the

Bible to be visible or even to be read in his presence. I took our children to church over his objections and attended Bible Study Fellowship for a number of years until I started working full time at the family business. During this time my relationship with Christ, my church attendance, and my long-distance calls to my mother strengthened me.

Over time, Hal softened somewhat in his objections to my faith. In 1979, he was arrested for driving under the influence of alcohol, with an added charge of assault with a deadly weapon. That night, after bailing him out of jail, I was able to persuade him to read a booklet called "The 4 Spiritual Laws." I pray that he truly meant the words that he repeated. His life didn't ever reflect a great change, although he did attend Challenger's Sunday School with Glenn Schaeffer for quite a few years. In 2005 he chose to be baptized by our son CJ, who was a pastor.

Hal passed away in 2015 with dementia, leaving behind three children, 15 grandchildren, and six great-grandchildren. I am so richly blessed by my family.

At the age of 82, I look back on my long life and have such a strong feeling of gratitude to my Savior for all of my blessings. Watching my children, grandchildren, and great-grandchildren grow and learn from their trials, mistakes and successes shows just how important it is to make wise choices.

Key Scripture

My life's verse is Romans 8:28 which says, "And we know that God causes everything to work together for the good of those who love God and are called according to His purpose for them." This verse was such a comfort and held me together through some very rough times.

Walking with Jesus has been the source of my strength. My prayer for my beloved family is that each one will reach out to Him through prayer and the studying of His precious word.

Martha Cavillo Juslin

You Will Never Be Alone

I am one of six children, the only girl among five brothers, and I had a very dysfunctional upbringing. As a result, I grew up always feeling unloved, rejected, abused, and emotion-ally and spiritually neglected. This is how my mind was set from the very beginning.

I know now that parents cannot give to their children what they themselves do not possess but I didn't know that then and I was hurt and angry with the dynamics of my family. So, there I am, with a label and message in my head that I was there to serve and clean and endure whatever the males desired. Unfortunately, starting with my father, drinking alcohol was the focus for fun. With the drinking came dad's sketchy friends. They would come to our home unannounced and steal all the family time. This was allowed because my parents didn't want, or know how, to say no! No to unwanted company, no to allowing our home to be the hangout. So, as a result, the streets were where the kids lived; South of Market, San Francisco between 6th and 7th streets.

I was dominated by fear, surrounded by drunks, pedophiles, addicts and abused women and families. Before I was out of elementary school I was already sniffing glue, smoking and drinking a little alcohol. Molestation began at age 8 and lasted until age 14 when my family finally moved.

By the time I'd graduated from high school I had already been beaten repeatedly by a drunk father, ridiculed by family and close family friends, and ignored and frowned upon by my mother. Looking for anyone to pay attention, I cried out to God, "Don't you see me?"

Fast forward to my only boyfriend in high school. He was mentally, physically and sexually abusive. I was so insecure and had no self-worth. I moved to Texas to get away from him. Still, looking for love and peace, I married a man from Texas, thinking he'd be everything different than my culture and upbringing and we'd find a better way of living. Nope, he too was broken and unfaithful, so, I moved back to San Francisco. There, another man pays attention to me and there I go again, actually believing we were gonna show this world and our families how happiness is done. Wrong again. He was just another broken individual, but this time we had started attending church.

So, we had the church to help, right? Wrong! Who wants to get their lives involved with such toxicity and dysfunction? No one! Unfortunately, I learned that attending church doesn't just fix everything and other Christians, even leaders, are not always equipped or available. And let's face it, sometimes they're not even willing to get involved in another person's problems.

Nonetheless, I committed to trying to fit in, trying to learn to "Let go and let God" but still it seemed that no one was willing to become "our church family" or to take us under their wings and light the way. I searched for counseling for us, but my husband only gave lip service with no real intention of implementing change.

Then in 2013, I heard God's call to me! I was lying on the floor, curled up from crying, and God said, " Stop arguing with him. You are participating in more sin that way. Be still and know that I Am God, and go enjoy your day and tell everyone what I've done for you."

I began to trust in God alone! I moved away from defeat and hostility and also received spiritual counseling. I removed myself from the toxicity and joined the 3Crosses choir and began a new life of worship and praise in the midst of my turmoil. Now I know that God is my only hope and He has lifted my head and given me peace that passes understanding. He has freed me of the life I once lived, a life apart from Him, and now I have a new and joyful life walking with Him daily.

God told me to live and to leave my family in His hands. As for me, I needed to get away in order to heal and recover and discover what God has intended for me in this life from the beginning. So for now, I am on the Potter's wheel, loving the transformation, from old to new, His wonderful work in progress. God will get—and has—all the glory.

For the Next Generation

As I finish my testimony, I know that God wants my story to speak to the next generation. So, I say look for God first and foremost, because he's looking for you! He has a beautiful life in store even with troubles and heartaches. He knows what's best. He made you. Trust his Living Word and the people who have been transformed by it. Don't waste time going your own way, hurting yourself and others along the way because you think you need to be in control and grown up. No, we are always children of God. Stay dependent on Him and His ways, like a child, and know God is our perfect parent, who will always be there, guiding and filling life with His great adventure and fullness. You will never be alone.

The other thing I want to say is that in my old life, I started out a victim of my feelings and as an alien and stranger among my family. But thanks be to God! In my new life I am a victor in Christ alone and can trust the feelings of the Holy Spirit to be a saved stranger, alien, and pilgrim looking for a " New City" and "Eternal Home." Now I am confident in the journey and in what His Love, joy, peace, patience, kindness, goodness, gentleness, faithfulness and self-control will create in me for His glory.

Key Scriptures

"For the law of the Spirit of Life has set you free in Christ Jesus from the law of sin and death."

- ROMANS 8:2

"For He chose us in Him before the creation of the world to be holy and blameless in His sight."

- EPHESIANS 1:4

"The Lord will give strength to his people, the Lord will bless his people with peace."

- PSALM 29:11

"You are a chosen people, a royal priesthood, a holy nation, a people belonging to God, that you may declare the praises of Him who called you out of darkness into His marvelous light."

- 1 PETER:2:9

"Show me your ways O LORD, teach me your paths, guide me in your truths and teach me. For you are God my Savior and my hope is in you all the day long."

- PSALM 25:4-5

Marty Barnikel

Thy Will be Done

I was born in Oklahoma but grew up in Santa Rosa, California, one of 4 children. Mom and Dad were both teachers—Dad in high school and Mom in grammar school.

My parents were Christians, and involved members of the Santa Rosa Methodist Church so all four of us kids attended church. Even though I was active in the Sunday Schools and Methodist Youth Fellowship, I didn't really hear the gospel preached until my late 30's. In the meanwhile, I had lived an undirected life in which I made poor life decisions, such as marrying at the age of 22 without giving it much thought, and four years later getting pregnant, which wasn't in my husband's plans. That marriage ended in divorce by the time my son was one-year old.

Five years later, I married a man who lived in Washington State and we began attending a church that preached the gospel and had altar calls after each service.

It was at this church where I was baptized and became a member. However, even though I had confessed Jesus as my Lord and Savior, I had no idea of what that really meant. As a result, operating under my own power, I enthusiastically proceeded to volunteer for any and all opportunities to serve. At this time, I was teaching during the days, which limited my daytime Bible studies. But faithfully, God opened the opportunity for me to join the very first evening meetings of Bible Study Fellowship, held in nearby Mercer Island. This 5-year in-depth Bible Study grounded me in my faith.

During this time, it seemed that life was going well. However, when my son was 16 years old, my marriage started to fall apart, and after seeking counseling we agreed to a divorce. Soon after, my son came down with an illness that lasted for several months. It was a long and agonizing period of time before we saw any progress and it wasn't until I finally turned him over to the Lord and prayed, "Thy will be done," that my son was healed. Ever since then, my life has been guided by the knowledge that God loves me and desires my very best. All He wants from me is to trust and obey Him.

After my son graduated from high school and began his college years, I felt God's strong hand leading me to something new. In 1984 when I was a member of our church's Missions Council, I learned that teachers were needed in China to teach English to Chinese college students. Earlier, I had taken a trip to tour Mainland China with my mother, and while there I felt drawn to the country and its people in a most supernatural way. So after praying and following through the doors that God opened for me, I discovered a Christian organization in Southern California that would train and place English teachers in colleges throughout China. With the support of my church, I made application to the organization and was accepted for the school year 1985-86. I then took a leave of absence from my community college and taught for a year in Changchun, China. It was a year that was much blessed with spiritual growth and new visions for my life.

During that year, I felt God's prompting to commit to longer service in China, but to do so meant I needed to get more training in teaching English. So, while still in China, I applied to the Master's degree program of Teaching English to Speakers of Other Languages (TESOL) at the University of Washington in Seattle, took my GRE test in China with hundreds of hopeful Chinese students, and eagerly awaited the results. On getting the news I had been accepted, I immediately resigned my position at the community college.

When I returned to Seattle, I had no place to live, but as God would have it, he had prepared a home for me in advance. A friend with whom I had taught in the community college heard that I was returning to the States and planning to begin studies at the University of Washington. She and her husband, both strong Christians, had just built a house close to the University with plans to accommodate nine visiting scholars from Mainland China. All had been prepared, but they needed a Christian to manage the home. Enter Marty. I joyfully lived with the scholars and managed the home for two and one half years. This was indeed a gift from God that met my needs to serve the Chinese as well as to study for my degree-—a win-win.

I received my Master's degree in 1988, which was the same year my son graduated from Palmer Chiropractic College. All seemed to be a "go" for me to return to China to continue my goal of teaching English there. However, God had other ideas. In the course of my making plans to go to China, I received a phone call from the director of a nonprofit Christian organization in Berkeley, California. She said she needed someone to help her in the administration of her relatively new China teacher-sending organization and asked if I would like to move to the Bay Area and become Assistant Director.

Even though I wanted to go back to China, God moved my heart to accept the position. God's reason for this became clear shortly thereafter. My parents, who still lived in Santa Rosa, had been in poor health and were being cared for by my youngest brother who lived nearby in Rohnert Park. Sadly, ten days after I accepted the position in Berkeley, my brother was killed in a boating accident, making it necessary for me to see after my parents. Praise God for His care and perfect timing.

While working at ERRC I met my German husband, Dietmar, who was a prominent chef in San Francisco and, coincidentally, on the Board of Directors of ERRC. We found that we had common interests and both loved the Lord so, after a rather short courtship, we were married in 1993. Since then we have traveled extensively both for fun and for Christian service and have served Him wherever we were called at 3Crosses. We are thankful that God has been central to our marriage these past 28 years, as He has carried us through many of life's challenges and has blessed us with joy.

My advice to younger generations is to learn about God by studying His precious Word and spending personal time with Him on a daily basis. Always consult Him before making decisions. You can trust Him, for He is faithful.

Key Scriptures

Trust in the Lord with all your heart and lean not on your own understanding. In all your ways, submit to him and He will make your paths straight.

- PROVERBS 3:5-6

And we know that in all things God works for the good of those who love him, who have been called according to his purpose.

- ROMANS 8:28

I can do all things through Christ who strengthens me.

- PHILIPPIANS 4:3

The Lord is my shepherd, I shall not want.

- PSALMS 23:1

Mary Whitfield

Lead the Lost to Christ

I thank God I grew up in a loving and peaceful family with my parents, three brothers and two sisters. I loved hearing Bible stories in school about The Creation, Adam and Eve, Noah, Jesus and all the miracles He performed in showing His love to people. I believed Jesus was God's son and that He loved all people including me. I knew He died on the cross, was buried, rose from the grave and ascended to heaven.

But I didn't understand the details of the true gospel message which most people know, "For God so loved the world, that He gave His only begotten Son, that whoever believes in Him should not perish but have eternal life:" - John 3:16

I also didn't understand John 1:12, which says, "...to those who received Him [Jesus], to those who believed in His name, He gave the right to become children of God."

I had never heard Romans 6:23..."The wages of sin is death [hell] but the gift of God is eternal life [Heaven] through Jesus Christ our Lord."

I also had never heard 2 Corinthians 5:21," God made Him [Jesus] to be sin for us, who knew no sin, so that we might become the righteousness of God in Him."

Jesus Himself made the gospel very clear by saying, "I am the Way, the Truth, the Life. No one comes to the Father except through me."

I figured I surely would go to Heaven someday because I loved God and tried to keep the commandments. But, not so. The Bible says in Ephesians 2:8-9 that we "are saved by grace...through faith....and this is not from ourselves, it is the gift of God not by works lest anyone should boast."

Well, life moved on. In my late teens, I thought the best goal in life was to be happily married, to have children and to do fun things together as a family. Every night I prayed, "Lord, help me to have a happy and successful marriage." Well, a few years later I got married, and as in many marriages, my husband and I had struggles.

It was during one of those difficult times when my sister connected with me. She shared the gospel message and how the Lord was working in her life and got me involved. I went with her to Neighborhood Church (now 3 Crosses) and to a Bible study at a friend's house. I went home and read "The 4 Spiritual Laws" booklet, which the leader there had given me, and learned how to become a child of God. I prayed, admitted to God that I was a sinner, asked Him to forgive my sins and to come into my life to be my Lord and Savior. And He did! Oh what joy!

Very soon after that, I joined Bible Study Fellowship (BSF), plus a home Bible study and a weekly prayer meeting in the home of someone I considered my spiritual mother. I was amazed at all the truth I was learning and grew closer to God every day. I was so thrilled that He was living in me, that He would never leave me, that He would supply all my needs according to His riches in Christ Jesus and that the moment I took my last breath on this earth I would live with Him in Heaven! I wanted to shout it from a mountain top so everyone could know the joys of being God's child!

Since that time, my marriage has seen great changes for the good, which I thank God abundantly for. Among these blessings were my husband coming to Christ and our re-marriage after a brief divorce. The Lord blessed us with two wonderful children, our son-in-law and two grandsons.

Some years ago, I discovered in a class that my personal life mission is "to glorify God by leading the lost to Christ and helping those in need." I have served the Lord in various ways since becoming a Christian. It was my joy to do so then and still is. In recent years I have been involved in the church kitchen ministry and in children's ministry leadership at Community Bible Study (CBS). I also hand out tracts, help individuals in various ways, and above all, follow the verse that says to "Always be prepared to give an answer to everyone who asks you to give the reason for the hope you have." (2 Peter 3:15) God has truly been good to me, and I am thankful He is helping me to live the abundant life that Jesus came to give me.

I would advise everyone, no matter your age or how good or bad you feel you are or have been, that the most important decision you can make is to believe in Jesus and receive Him as your Lord and Savior. Then walk faithfully with Him in obedience to His commands and trust His promises.

Like the vertical and horizontal spokes on a smoothly running wheel, it's important for spiritual growth to read God's word, pray to Him, fellowship with believers and share the gospel with 'the world."

Key Scriptures

Live out Proverbs 3:5-6. "Trust in the Lord with all your heart, lean not on your own understanding, in all your ways acknowledge Him and He will direct your path." I love using Romans 12:12 as a helpful focus. "Be joyful in hope, patient in affliction, faithful in prayer." And remember, God is faithful to His promises. He is our help and strength at all times!

Mary Wong

The Lucky 12

I became a Christian when introduced to church in Junior High. My parents belonged to a group called The Lucky 12 which consisted of a dozen couples. A different couple hosted the group each month as they got together for fun games of mahjong (the wives) and poker (the husbands).

Some couples brought their families with them and the kids would mingle on their own. I was one of them and there was another girl my age. The man's daughter went to church and my dad thought it would be a good idea for me even though he never went. He thought it would be a good place for me to socialize.

My parents arranged a sleep-over at the other girl's house and the next morning, her dad took me to church with his daughter. She introduced me around the small, apartment-like church and I saw another friend and a cousin I knew. I went a couple of times. Then, one night when a Lucky 12 party was at our house, the other girl brought a tract to share with me.

We sat on the side of the bed and read the tract together and that was when I accepted Jesus Christ as my Savior.

My parents worked and attended those parties but never attended church. We just co-existed in the same house but every once in a while, I could talk with my dad, who would stop what he was doing and just listen. My mom and dad made sure that I was well-provided for.

That small church was very friendly. They had weekly clubs for kids from elementary all the way to college. The children always had guidance through their teaching and events and the church provided the transportation with the many vans they purchased. I had no social problems and there was always something to chat about to someone.

While growing up and dealing with all the worldly challenges, I was in groups that centered on the Lord. The groups had annual meetings where the boys and girls met separately to talk about anything they wanted to regarding growing up. I didn't have to worry about peer pressure, drugs or joining a gang. I had a Lord-centered group and church was the most positive thing in my life.

Was it church or was it the Lord Himself who kept me coming back? I believe it was those who the Lord touched to serve Him in capacities of club sponsors, drivers, counselors, pastors and speakers.

I found out about a God who cares, among billions of people, about me. A God who cares about my identity in Him, my confidence in Him, my attitudes, my actions -- that they would reflect His goodness and love, which is beyond what the world could give me.

My God has other attributes that attract me to Him. Not only is He good, gracious and loving when the world isn't, He is glorious, holy, merciful, just and faithful even when I am not. He is self-sufficient—it is only because of His love I can have eternal life, not because of anything I've done in my life. He is wise beyond all human thinking, all-powerful, all-knowing, everywhere— there isn't any place He is not.

All I had to do was to say I believe in His Son, Jesus Christ, that He died on the cross to pay for my sin and ask Him to come into my life.

I would like to share the need to search for God with my children and grandchildren. Find Him and His Son Jesus and join a God-honoring group, a community of believers that studies the Bible and helps you grow through life's circumstances. If your church provides it, find a mentor, someone who is impartial and mature in the Lord. Find a person you can spend time with and provide the opportunity to share the things you struggle with.

One of my favorite songs is Waymaker, which describes the character of God. Life is not always pleasant. When things happen, focus on the song and you will find peace.

Key Scriptures

Ephesians 1:3-14 describes our identity in Christ. In the world, you will get huge amounts of criticism and teasing from others. You will get many self-judgements from yourself. Some of these can be harmful to a healthy self. Many are lies the world has taught you to believe about yourself. Now, look at what Christ tells about you. Those are true! That's God saving you from harmful thoughts.

Ephesians 3:14-21 describes God's riches, strength, love. God is vast. God is more than what we humans can ever imagine.

My wish to anyone who reads this is that you find strength, peace, hope and a relationship with Jesus Christ.

Mike Absher

Look for the Truth

I was not raised in a Christian home, even though as a very young boy I went to Sunday School through a bus ministry. My early interests and life's career path revolved around science and sports. Science taught me and repeatedly stated that there is no God. That very same science made it clear that God and science are mutually exclusive, they do not mix. With no involvement with God in my home life, no allowance for God in school, and my work in a scientific field where God was denied, I definitely declare that "God truly works in wondrous ways." So, you might wonder how I became such a strong and bold Christian. This is how it occurred.

It became clear to me, after many years falsely denying God's existence, that He is alive! In fact, He was present all my life, even though I denied Him. God's persistence and presence, by the power of the Holy Spirit, continued to seek me, until I fell on my knees before Him and confessed Jesus as my Lord and Savior.

As a scientist I proposed this question to myself. Did I create myself? No, of course not! My parents came together and I became, right? No, not just biology, there had to be more! Simply put, where did I come from? Who made Me, Michael? Who gave me a soul and a spirit? Are all those the same question? Are there any answers to those age old questions? Did I just come out of the nothing or did I just evolve? No!

The only thing science gave me were many empty answers or, at least, more questions. Those answers do not explain one fact. I do have a being, my spirit. More than biology, more than evolution, which don't explain spirit. Science and biology, and certainly not evolution, were not the answer! In fact, I came from someone, from somewhere else, something more. Yes! Someone gave me "the spirit of life." I wasn't just cells that grew inside my mother.

Science could tell the processes of birth and all that entails, but it could never answer the big questions like, where did the universe come from or when did it begin? When does the life force come into those cells inside my mom? There must be an answer, a starting point, because things don't just happen without a starting point! I could not come up with an answer.

When I was at the lowest point in my dissatisfied and destructive life, I listened. I finally HEARD, not my conscience or Jiminy Cricket, but "that voice inside of me telling me to mend my family and look for truth." I knew for certain I couldn't do it myself. Yes, that ever-present voice which had always been inside of me finally got through!

Even so, ever defiant, I asked, why do I need to go to church? No answer! It took me some days fighting but I wanted answers. So, after nearly 33 years of denial, I went back to church where my wife, who was not a church person, had retreated for protection. I joined her and our sons and that inner voice I had ignored and denied all of my life spoke loudly through my hurts. It said, "I am here, just believe, trust and come find rest under my wings."

In 1994, on my knees, I asked Jesus to guide my life as Lord and Savior. I had begun to reconcile with my second wife and my children and some Christian counseling helped greatly. I listened and began to grow in my knowledge of the Lord!

I know why God allowed me to explore the falsehoods science offers and why evolution as taught in our schools today is wrong. God allowed me to walk down wrong paths so I could counsel and teach others who had questions and no answers. If you have any of these same questions, feel free to ask me for more info or further clarification. I am happy to discuss these truths further.

But just realize this. As always, when science finds a better truth they just rewrite the textbooks and proclaim those other, older scientists got it wrong. Sorry! On the other hand, have you noticed that our Bible is re-translated, researched and reviewed but the basic religious doctrine or tenets are unchanged? I wonder why.

I implore anyone who reads this to please listen to the voice that beckons from "within and without" each of us!

I affirm that my justification is by grace alone through faith alone because of Christ alone. In justification, Christ's righteousness is imputed to me as the only possible satisfaction of God's perfect justice.

I affirm that, because salvation is of God, for His glory, I must glorify him always.

I must live my entire life before the face of God, under the authority of God and for His glory alone.

I deny that I can properly glorify God if my worship is confused with entertainment, if I neglect either Law or Gospel in my teaching, or if self-improvement, self-esteem or self-fulfillment are allowed to become alternatives to the Gospel.

Jesus is the sustainer of my daily walk and the finisher of my spiritual journey. So, I thank God for His patience with me, and may the Grace and Peace of the Lord Reign in my life!

Finally, I am also sure of this, "He who began a good work in you will bring it to completion."

In Him you also heard the word of truth, the gospel "the good news of your salvation!"

Key Scripture

My life verse is Luke 11:53, which reads, "Woe to you experts in the law, because you have taken away the key to knowledge. You yourselves have not entered, and you have hindered those who were entering."

Mike Cavalleri

His Time, Not Mine

I heard about the Lord when I was in the Navy in 1960. During that time, I would go to the "Sing for Your Supper" meetings in Long Beach, CA. to get the free meals. I heard about Jesus during those meetings, but I ignored it. All I wanted was to do things for myself. When I got home from the Navy, I continued getting in trouble. I moved to San Francisco with my girlfriend, but that didn't work out. Then I met another woman and eventually married her, but that ended in divorce after about 11 years.

After the divorce, some dear friends, Harvey and Marie Klein, and their three children invited me to go to church to see their kids in a musical skit. Not knowing what the Lord had planned for me, I continued going to their church and a Sunday School class for adults. I was so lonely and had money troubles and other problems, and I lived in an 18-foot trailer for three years. During this time, as I continued to go to church, God softened my heart. I finally gave in and accepted Jesus Christ as my Savior.

I hadn't wanted to give up a life of sin because I thought going to church would take away my fun and freedom. But as a Christian, I've discovered a life that is so much fun. It turns out I didn't give up fun and freedom at all. As time went on, I started turning my problems over to Him. Things began to slowly improve but I had to learn that all things come in His time, not mine.

In the Sunday School class I was attending, there was a group of people who were not married. We would go out to dinner on Sunday evenings, which was often the highlight of my week. I decided to ask one of the ladies in this group to go with me to a yearly picnic event held at a camp near Watsonville, CA. I was as nervous as a high school kid when asking her for a date. It was wonderful when she accepted. On the way home from the picnic, we stopped in Capitola to walk on the beach. At one point I took her hand to help her across a creek that was running out to the ocean, and when we held hands, we both knew there was something special in our relationship. The Lord put Nancy Francis into my life. He had definitely put us together.

A few months later, my dear friends, the Kleins and their three beautiful children, decided to go to Disneyland in their motorhome. I had a pickup truck with a camper, so Nancy and I decided to go, too. On the way to Disneyland, Nancy rode with me. She would sleep in the motorhome with the Kleins and their son would stay with me. I loved her so much that, during the drive, I asked her to marry me and she said yes. I knew that the Lord was in charge. I wondered how He could put together two different people like us, but felt this was what He wanted and who am I to ask why? We have been married 37 years, and we have one wonderful son. Over the years God has guided us through some big problems, including financial issues, lost jobs, and deaths of family members and friends. The Lord has taught me to pray and trust in Him through all of life's difficulties.

We began attending 3Crosses about 17 years ago. At that time, we felt that the Lord was leading us to find a new church. On Thanksgiving weekend that year, Nancy's parents were visiting us. We told her mom that we wanted to try out 3Crosses Church, and she said, "Let's go." So we did, and we've never left. We felt so welcome here and knew this was where the Lord wanted us.

One thing I wanted to do was to serve others as an usher. The Lord led me to Bob Okamura, who was the Head Usher at that time. I worked under his guidance for a few years and when he retired, the Lord led me to take his place as Head Usher. It was such a wonderful experience serving the Lord in that way.

Susan Okamura was a leader of a Bible Study small group and the Lord guided us to join that group. I did not read very well at all so one of the first things I told Susan was that I didn't want to read or pray out loud. Well, the Lord took over again, and Susan asked me to read just one verse out loud. I had time to read the verse to myself several times before it was my turn to read out loud, making sure I knew all the words. That was the beginning of God helping me improve my reading skills. He has caused such an improvement that, as of this time, I have read through the Bible eight times, and am currently reading through a chronological Bible. Praise God for teaching me to read so well and for giving me enjoyment in reading and learning His Word. I praise Him for helping me to read His Word!

I feel so fortunate to have met and worked with some wonderful pastors and to have made some life-long friends here at 3Crosses. My wonderful wife of 37 years has been a very special blessing to me. We know that what we do is always with the Lord's help.

In closing, I accepted the Lord in September, 1980, and wish I had done it so much earlier in my life. I just turned 78 years old and have had a wonderful life with the Lord. Even though I have had some problems, I have nothing to complain about. I know that by turning my problems over to the Lord in prayer, He has accomplished so much in my life. No matter what comes your way, pray to the Lord continuously and wait for Him to guide you through.

You don't need to feel lost in a large church like 3Crosses. Join a small group and do some volunteer work in the church. You can also become part of one of the community classes. As you become involved in these groups, you could meet some wonderful people that will become life long friends. God will bless you greatly as you draw close to Him.

Key Scripture

My favorite Scripture is still John 3:16. "For God so loved the world that He gave his one and only Son, that whoever believes in Him shall not perish but have eternal life."

Nancy Besson

With the Love of the Lord

My siblings and I were sent to Sunday Sch-ool as children. My younger brother and I went to a church-sponsored summer ca-mp when I was around ten, and it was there that I gave my heart to the Lord.

In my teens and twenties, I strayed away from the Lord, and it is by the grace of God that I lived through those years. I didn't go on to college right out of high school and at age 21, I met my future husband, Wayne.

Wayne was raised in the church but strayed away during his senior year of college. He taught Philosophy at a university and became involved in The God Is Dead Movement. He tried to convince me there was no God, but I never gave in. However, since my teens, I had already decided that I didn't need Jesus.

We married in 1972 when I was 25 and when Wayne said he didn't want children, I agreed. He already had a son from his first marriage. But, I became pregnant in 1975, despite our using precautions. Wayne wanted me to have an abortion, but I refused. Our marriage was really rocky until my seventh month, when he finally came around.

Laurie was born with two heart defects and needed two surgeries, one when she was at 3-1/2 months and another at 20 months. I began praying to God, but still didn't connect the need for Jesus.

In 1976, Wayne lost his job, and we moved in with his parents in Omaha, Nebraska. I didn't know anything about alcoholism, but Wayne drank a lot and became an alcoholic. Of all things, we bought the largest nightclub in Omaha and my life became a living hell.

Our second daughter, Nicole, was born in 1977 and we got our own apartment. I remember my sister, Laurine, would call me once a week and I would cry. Her family lived in northern California and she had become a born-again Christian a few years before. She would tell me each time she called that I needed Jesus. I told her that I was too bad of a sinner and I owned a bar so I wasn't worthy. My sister witnessed to me that we are all sinners and that none of us are worthy but we are saved by grace.

Wayne intimidated me, so I took my two girls and flew to Laurine's with the intention of surrendering my life to Christ. On Sunday, March 26, 1978, the pastor of Laurine's church gave an invitation and I gave my heart to Christ. I was much bolder and confident when I returned home and started attending my in-law's church. It was very small, but they had recently begun a 12-week discipleship program. God's timing was perfect.

Fast forward to Christmas 1985. We were living in Los Angeles and my parents came down from the Bay Area to visit. My mother announced that she had become a born-again

Christian. My father intimidated her like Wayne had intimidated me. My mother said that she wished she could see her grandchildren more often but in October 1986 she was diagnosed with cancer and seven days later she died.

My daughter Laurie had kidney failure at age 9 and was on kidney dialysis, which I gave her at home. Wayne and I were separated at the time and Laurie was put on a list for a kidney transplant. But in January 1985, he gave his heart to Christ and went through an alcohol treatment program. I didn't love Wayne in my humanness, but I kept asking God to let me love him with the love of the Lord. We got back together as a family and renewed our vows in March 1985.

During the Thanksgiving 1986 weekend, we were at Wayne's parents' house. On Friday, November 28, Laurie told Grandma Shirbroun that she was going to faint, but she died. We were out in the country, on their farm, so we didn't wait for an ambulance. We drove her to the hospital where she was brain dead. I tried to give Laurie CPR, to no avail. We called her cardiologist and he told us she died without pain. Laurie adored Grandma Shirbroun and I believe she was where she wanted to be when the Lord took her to heaven. This happened about 5 weeks after my mother had passed away. God answered my mother's prayer by having her wait for Laurie in heaven.

When parents lose a child, no matter the age, they either draw closer to God or away from Him. I drew closer to God, but Wayne drew away. He returned to drinking and we divorced. He died of cancer on Christmas Eve, 2007, at the age of 67. Wayne never gave up drinking, but I believe he got right with God near the end.

I am 74 now, and I think I could fill a book with how God has blessed me and shown his love for me. Jesus is with me every day of my life. The Holy Spirit is inside me as my guide and comforter. My daughters and my sons-in-law walk close with the Lord. My two grandchildren, ages 15 and 9, accepted Jesus as their savior and were recently baptized.

In the name of Jesus, Amen and Amen.

Nina Filler

The Lord's Love Never Ends

I have early memories of attending church with my mother. These memories were during World War II in Europe so I remember hiding in a ditch during an air raid as we walked to church.

As a teenager in post-war Germany my family attended a Lutheran church. In 1948, I was attending a youth fellowship outreach group by the Christian and Missionary Alliance. These missionaries from Canada held bible teaching Sunday school classes and fellowship activities. It was during this time period when my mother, Magdalena, accepted Jesus as her Lord and began a lifetime of growing in study and discipleship.

Through these missionaries I came to attend a summer camp. On July 27th, 1953 I accepted Jesus as my savior at summer camp in the Harz mountains. Years later, I was baptized by Pastor Mark Teyler in the Jordan River.

During my formative times as a young adult and a young believer, I remember teachings on the importance of knowing that God was always watching what we do and what we say. God is also listening to our prayers and it was never too early to begin praying for my future husband. I spent two years in confirmation classes where we would memorize entire chapters of Scripture. Much of this is still impacting me even years later, having a foundation of God's word that is always there to draw upon.

I grew up hearing and loving classic hymns, the beautiful words and melodies that are always with you in times of joy and apprehension. One or two lines from a beloved hymn can lead to hours of personal praise. I am grateful for the early foundation in Scripture and hymn worship that I received when I was still a youth.

I came to the United States when I was 18-years of age. My family was sponsored by a Lutheran Church in San Leandro and after a lengthy three-year process we came through New York Harbor and flew to our new home in California.

I did pray for my future husband and was blessed that God had chose a wonderful man for me in the U.S. We were married for 35 wonderful years, and my priorities were my husband and my children. With the demands of a young family, it was often difficult to find the time and closeness I wanted with the Lord. I would often remember a song from my youth group days and the line, "give of your best to the Lord." I wanted to do more and what I could do should be my best.

Key Scripture

After 35 years of marriage the Lord took my husband home after a sudden and quick illness. During this tough time, I read

Lamentations 3:21-23 over and over. "But this I call to mind, and therefore I have hope: The steadfast love of the Lord never ceases; his mercies never come to an end: they are new every morning: great is your faithfulness." God's mercies are new and refreshing now and every morning because He is faithful. It may hurt right now but God is present and bringing newness.

I grew much closer to the Lord during this time of transition and began another season as a caregiver to my aging mother who was suffering from dementia. My 501 mission-statement was "to serve the Lord with a joyful heart." During this demanding stage I needed the constant reminder to be patient and joyful, especially on challenging days when there was little patience to be found. Joy does not come from circumstances but from times of closeness with the Lord. "Softly and Tenderly" Jesus is always calling us closer to Him. During all of life's seasons and stages I can say, "Thank you Lord for saving my soul" and for always being faithful to me.

Patricia Monk

We Live Through Him

I didn't come from a church-going family but was allowed and later encouraged to attend Sunday school and church. When I was 5 years old, I went to Sunday school with our neighbor in Altadena, California. My family moved to Hayward when I was 8 years old, and my sisters and I started attending a small Bible believing church. When I was about 10 years of age, I accepted Christ as my Lord and Savior.

When I was a freshman in high school, my family moved again to Fullerton, California, where my sisters and I became active in Youth for Christ. Bob Kraning was our youth leader and we grew a lot under his leadership. We especially enjoyed being members of a Bible quiz team that forced us to study the scriptures.

When I was a senior in high school, my family moved to Oakland. Even though my parents didn't attend, my father went to meet with Jake Bellig at Neighborhood Church. Jake told him that the church could use their help at the Port of

Call. So, I soon became a hostess at the Port of Call, coached a Junior High Girls Basketball team and teamed up to teach Sunday School with a handsome guy named Butch Monk.

I knew Butch was the one God had chosen for me and we were married on August 22, 1970. Ours was the first wedding at the new church in Castro Valley. Soon after we were married, my father passed away suddenly at the age of 46. The became the impetus for my mother to start attending church and become a Christian. Praise the Lord!

We have been blessed with four children and fifteen grandchildren. Our greatest desire is for them to see Jesus in us and to know how much He loves them.

I would like to pass on that God is faithful even though we stray at times. He has rescued me from a few bad choices. Praise to Him.

It's also important that we don't listen to the devil's lies. He always wants to malign God's character, which is why it is so important to pray and read the Bible every day. We can pray about everything, not holding back our thoughts and concerns. We can be honest with God!

Key Scripture

Philippians 4:4-7 says, "Rejoice in the Lord always. I will say it again: Rejoice! Let your gentleness be evident to all. The Lord is near. Do not be anxious about anything, but in every situation, by prayer and petition, with thanksgiving, present your requests to God. And the peace of God, which transcends all understanding, will guard your hearts and your minds in Christ Jesus."

I also turn to 1 John 4:9-11, which says, "This is how God showed his love among us: He sent His one and only Son into the world that we might live through Him. This is love not that we loved God, but that He loved us and sent His Son as an atoning sacrifice for our sins. Dear friends, since God so loved us, we also ought to love one another."

Paulette Richardson

Don't Neglect Prayer

I have been a Christian since I was 12 years old. I babysat for the couple across the street from us. They took me to their church in Bakersfield and I accepted the Lord there.

My mother's father was a minister. My father's father was a minister. Maybe that is why they did not go to church but they always let my brother and I go to any church we wanted to attend. I have always attended church no matter where we lived. If a church was close to us, we went there. If a bus came by, we went to that church. I was baptized at a church in Alameda when I was in high school. They took us to Oakland to see Billy Graham and I rededicated my life there and began to grow in the Lord.

What I want the next generation to know is that your Christian life is not easy and it's not a straight line. Don't give up, but continue to grow. Read your Bible every day and memorize scripture that speaks to you.

Key Scripture

My favorite verse is John 1:1. "In the beginning was the Word. And the Word was with God and the Word was God." It means that the Word was Jesus. He always was, is, and is to come. You can pray to Him each and every day and all day long.

Did you pray about it? It's the first thing you should do when you have a problem, whether it is as simple as, "where did I put ......? or if you're looking for a parking space, or praying about kids or siblings. When you tell someone you will pray for them, please pray; don't forget about it. When God tells you to pray for someone and brings them to your mind, pray for that person. You never know why God told you to pray for them. You may never know, but pray anyway.

Peter Zacharoff

A Life of Teaching

Peter was born in Kaiserslautern, Germany. His mom won the lottery to come to America, and the family settled in Bellevue, Washington.

He was an altar boy in the Catholic Church in Washington State for 10 years before joining the U.S. Army. He was stationed in Texas, got saved at a Christian Servicemen's Center and later became a chaplain's assistant. He also served as a tour guide for American servicemen and women stationed in Germany.

After the Army, Peter attended Bible school and met his wife, Debbie, at a Christian College. They were married by Dr. Jacob Bellig at Neighborhood Church in Castro Valley.

Peter attended seminary, then earned his master's in Special Education. He taught at Fremont Christian School for 10 years, then at Redwood Christian School for seven years. He is now a public school Special Education Teacher and a member of the Hayward Gideons camp.

Randy Odom

God Pushed "Play"

"Now to him who is able to do immeasurably more than all we ask or imagine, according to his power that is at work within us, to him be glory in the church and in Christ Jesus throughout all generations, for ever and ever! Amen." - Ephesians 3:20-21

I was born in Tulsa, Oklahoma on July 27, 1957 and am my parents' only child. My mom, Julia (aka Jude), had a daughter named Pamela Jo Odom who was stillborn three years before I was born. Mom worked part-time as a concession manager at a local drive-in movie theater and as a restaurant manager. My dad, Richard, was a truck driver for the Katy (MK&T) Railroad from the time I was born until his retirement.

Ours was an average working-class life in the 1960's and 70's. Neither of my parents were churchgoers. My dad's parents divorced when he was young (something very unusual in Oklahoma in the 1940's), and my mom's father committed suicide when she was just a toddler. Consequently, both of my grandmothers had a difficult time raising their children on their own. Single mothers in those days were not commonplace in mainline society, much less in the church. Neither of my grandmothers felt welcomed or at-home in the church environment. I can say, though, that they raised their children as "cultural Christians," and I inherited that worldview from both of my parents.

At an early age I understood that there was a God, but beyond the cultural definition of that God, I had no understanding of His nature or of my relationship to Him. I remember sitting with my ear glued to the speaker of my parents' console stereo as Barbra Streisand sang "The Lord's Prayer" on a Christmas album. I felt goose bumps up and down my arms as I listened. I wondered who this "Father, which art in heaven" was that she sang so beautifully about.

By nature, I am a shy introvert. As a small child, with no brothers or sisters, I depended on neighbor children to be my friends. However, because I was so shy, I was afraid to go knock on their doors and ask them to come out and play with me. Instead, I would go out and sit on the curb by the street in front of my house and hope they would see me out there and come out to play. I was blessed, though, with some wonderful cousins who became like siblings to me. My dad's younger brother had a son just half-a-year younger than I, and we would often take turns spending the weekends at one another's homes. Little did I know that this ambiguous God that I believed in was unfolding His plan for me right before my eyes.

At around the age of 12, my uncle Ray became a Christian. The transformation of Christ in his life was truly miraculous. Now, on weekends when I would stay with their family, I would go to church with them. For the first time in my life I began to hear the story of the gospel explained and personalized for me. In 1972, just three months prior to my 15th birthday, I attended a Revival Fires Crusade with my uncle Ray and his family at the Tulsa Assembly Center. I had already been coming under the conviction of the Holy Spirit when attending church with my uncle's family, so on this Thursday evening in April, when the invitation was given at the end of the message, I could no longer resist. I walked forward and gave my life to Jesus that night. Immediately following the crusade meeting a few of us went to a local church not far from my house and I was baptized into Christ. That began a transformation in my life that was astounding to my friends and family, and still astounds me as I look back on it.

I became actively involved in the high school youth group at East Tulsa Christian Church and the youth pastor there, David McClary, became my role model (dare I say idol?). I did everything I could to be like "Dave" and spent as much time with him as possible. I'm sure I made a pest of myself by hanging out at their house so much of the time after school and on summer days.

Dave had graduated from Ozark Christian College in Joplin, Missouri, so very early in my high school years I decided that I wanted to go to Ozark when I graduated. Sure enough, in 1975, after graduating from high school, I enrolled as a freshman at Ozark. I spent 4.5 wonderful years at Ozark, deepening my walk with Jesus and learning the skills of Christian leadership. In those days I had a decent singing voice and joined the concert choir. In my third year of college, this shy Okie boy found the courage to audition for an elite singing group on campus and I actually "made it!"

That year, 1977-1978, was another pivotal year in my life. The group, called the Impact Brass and Singers, toured all over the midwestern US during the school year and did an amazing three-month west coast tour during the summer of '78. I had been to visit relatives in southern California in my early childhood, but during that visit in the summer of '78, I fell in love with the Golden State. I secretly planted a dream in my heart of one day living here.

Once graduating from Bible College, I intended to go into local church ministry in some capacity. However, around that same time, my high school and college best friend, Chuck Foreman, decided that he was going to be a missionary. Our home church was an extremely mission-minded church, so I had heard many missionaries share their testimonies during seemingly endless slide presentations at Sunday evening services. However, I had absolutely no interest in ever being a missionary myself. I couldn't imagine myself dressing up in the local garb of the country where I served and then boring people to tears with my slide presen-tations. (Little did I know...!)

Chuck's decision to be a missionary made a huge impact on me and I started to wonder if perhaps God would call me in the same way. In the early 80's, just coming into vogue was the notion of using a secular career skill as a means of sharing the gospel in a country that was otherwise closed to traditional missions. Teaching English as a 2nd language was one such career that could open many doors to otherwise "closed countries" so this idea intrigued me very much.

Around that same time, a dear woman in my home church, Velva Jo Johnson, gave me a book about Hudson Taylor, a famous 19th century missionary to China. James Hudson Taylor founded the China Inland Mission in the 19th century. The CIM still exists today and is known as Overseas Missionary Fellowship. When I read the account of Taylor's commitment to the call God had on his life for China, I came away thinking, "I'm not even a Christian, much less a missionary!" With the Holy Spirit's conviction and the inspiration of Hudson Taylor's life, I began to think about going to China as an English teacher with the goal of sharing my faith with students and others.

In the summer of 1983, my secret dream of moving to California became a reality when I enrolled as a graduate student in the Department of TESOL (Teaching English to Speakers of Other Languages) at Biola University. By that time, my high school youth pastor had moved to Southern California to pastor a church in Rancho Cucamonga, so I moved in with his family while doing my study at Biola.

Sometime during the spring term of 1984, I found a flyer in my student mailbox from a Christian organization in Alhambra that was recruiting English teachers for Mainland China. Reflecting on my reading of Hudson Taylor's life, I had to inquire about the opportunity. Long story short, I applied and was accepted for the 1984-1985 academic year. After an eight week summer training program I was assigned to teach with two other guys in the city of Wuhan in central China. Needless to say, I had never even heard of Wuhan! But in August of 1984 my two teammates and I took off to faraway China to teach in the Wuhan Branch of the Chinese Academy of Sciences. Another trajectory-setting year was about to commence.

For the first semester in Wuhan, I was absolutely miserable. I had never felt so far away from home. In retrospect, I realize that I was suffering from what I now call "heart lag." My body was in China, but my heart was still in the USA. However, not long after the start of the second semester I began to make friends with some of my students and others, so that by the end of that first year I was ready to sign-on long term. I notified my sending organization that I would like to continue serving in China and they agreed that I could stay. What began as a one year commitment ended up as a six year stay and those six years were probably the most pivotal years of my life. This was when God grew in me a heart for missions and a commitment to finding my place in His mission plan.

Fast forward to the spring semester of 1991 when I was teaching in Zhongshan University in the southern city of Guangzhou in China. "ZhongDa" is one of the leading universities in south China and I had a wonderful experience that year. However, a botched romantic relationship sent me reeling emotionally and I decided at the end of that year to return to the States for a "break." The sending organization that I was with at that time had its home office in Berkeley and they asked if I would be willing to come back to the States and serve as their Director of Recruitment. I agreed because it would "keep my feet in China" while also giving me the chance to take a needed break from serving on the field.

In the summer of 1992, our organization had a summer training in Berkeley for new teachers going to China and I was involved as one of the trainers at that orientation. It was during that summer orientation that our office also welcomed a new clerical volunteer who had been a Taiwanese graduate student here in the States. Her name was Krystal and I remember being "smitten" by her pretty much from day one. Unfortunately, not only was Krystal not smitten by me, she even asked a mutual friend in our office why in the world I would sometimes clip roses from the neighborhood bushes and give them to her at the office. I was "crushed but not destroyed" by that comment and redoubled my efforts to show her my interest. Finally, the ice began to thaw and Krystal began to see how really irresistible I am!

We courted for three years and finally, when I was 38 years-old, we got married. By that time, I had left the China organization in Berkeley and had begun pastoring the Fruitvale Christian Church in Oakland. Krystal and I were married in that church in September of 1995. During our years at Fruitvale, we started what became a very successful English as a Second Language school as an outreach of the church. In its heyday our English school had more students than our church had members. Those were wonderful years; however, the stirring toward missions never left us and actually began to intensify in the early 2000's. In 2002 we resigned from our ministry in Oakland, not knowing where the Lord would send us next nor how He would provide for us.

At that time, I was in the job market and had mentioned to a friend who attended Neighborhood Church that I was looking for a job. She told me that she had recently seen an announcement in the church bulletin for a custodial position at the church. I asked for a phone number and decided to inquire. I remember meeting with Greg Patrick, the Facilities Manager at that time. After giving him a brief history of my life, he said, "Wow! We've never had anyone so overqualified apply for a janitorial position." He offered me the job at $1 per hour more than the job posting had listed and that was our first introduction to Neighborhood Church. Shortly after I started working at Neighborhood, Krystal and I attended a Sunday service for the first time. "Coincidentally" our first Sunday was "Missions Sunday" and our hearts were bursting! We walked out of the service that day saying, "We've found our church!" Again, little did we know...!

I worked as a custodian at Neighborhood for three months and then was hired by another organization sending Christian professionals to China, this one located in Hayward. As Director of Short-Term Programs, I was in charge of recruiting, training and leading short-term mission trips to China. While serving with this organization Krystal and I continued to attend Neighborhood and get more involved. Krystal joined the choir and I had a couple of opportunities to teach an elective class on missions. It was during this time that we got to know the pastoral staff a little more.

Around 2004, when Neighborhood Church did Rick Warren's "Purpose-Driven Life" study, I began to sense that familiar stirring in my spirit. One day I said to Krystal, "Wouldn't it be amazing if the Lord opened a door for me to serve at Neighborhood?" Being the wise woman she is, her response was, "Don't tell anyone, let's just pray!"

So we began praying that if it was God's will for us to serve at Neighborhood he would open the door in some way. Then one day I had a fateful lunch with Pastor Mark Teyler. (There'll be another fateful lunch a little later in my story, so hold on...) Mark invited me to go out to lunch with him to discuss another mission class he had invited me to teach. While at lunch Mark asked, "Randy, how long is your commitment with the organization you're serving now?" Wow, was that an open-door opportunity, or what? I felt the nudge of God's Spirit and replied, "Well, it's funny you should ask...." Then I explained to Mark what Krystal and I had been secretly praying about. After I shared with him, he said, "Randy, I'd love to bring you on staff if you're interested." I was like, "Am I interested?"

Well, in the fall of 2004 I came on staff part-time as Pastor of Outreach. I finished out my service with the China organization that year and joined the full-time pastoral staff of

Neighborhood Church in 2005. Again, God rocked our world with His goodness and His favor!

One of the things I have not mentioned up to now is the issue of my parents in these years. In the late 90's and early 2000's, as we started seeing my parents' health become more fragile and realized that we needed to be more involved in their care. Krystal actually made several extended trips to Oklahoma to help my parents when one or the other of them was hospitalized. We knew that even though they never said anything, they were secretly fearing that we were going to end up moving off to the outermost parts of the earth at a time when they were most in need of support and assistance. As a result, we came up with a "deal" for them.

On a trip back to Oklahoma we told them that we would agree to stay in the U.S. for the rest of their lives, if they would move to California rather than having us move to Oklahoma. Amazingly, they agreed. So, in the spring of 2003 my parents made the only major move of their lives and came to live in San Leandro. We were able to purchase a small home for them in the same neighborhood where we lived, and they were happy to be close to us. Unfortunately, that joy didn't last very long.

Exactly four months to the day from when they arrived in California, my dad passed away. He had been in failing health for the previous few months, so the adjustment was difficult for him. Once he was gone, my mom was stuck in a strange place where she had never lived and where she had no friends. After floundering for a good while regarding what was best for her, she ended up moving into Carlton Plaza Assisted Living in San Leandro. She thrived there until she passed in November of 2008. I'm delighted that, because my dad was a veteran of the Korean Conflict, we were able to bury both of my parents in the National Cemetery in Santa Nella, California.

After my parents passed away, Krystal and I looked at each other and said, "Well, we've fulfilled our commitment to Mom and Dad about staying in this country for the rest of their lives... now what?" By this time my role at Neighborhood had changed to Pastor of Connection and Krystal was thriving in an accounting position at a large non-profit in Oakland. We were both at the top of our game professionally and in every other way. Finally, after praying and thinking and talking a lot, we came to the peace of saying that while we were not actively looking for the "next assignment" in missions, we would keep our hearts open and "go" if we knew the Lord had called us. This became the posture of our hearts as the year 2009 dawned.

Now comes the time of the next fateful lunch. In January of 2009 I had lunch with Brian Kalsbeek at Chipotle in Castro Valley. We had gotten together just to hang out with no other agenda (or so we thought). As we talked, Brian began sharing with me about an organization he had gotten involved with in Cambodia. In fact, he was serving as Executive Director of this organization. As I listened, I said, "What are you talking about, Executive Director of a missions organization? You're a chiropractor, for crying out loud!" He chuckled and continued his story. As he excitedly shared with me the various projects of this organization he began to talk about an orphanage in the rural far north of the country. It was then, as I was taking a bite of my chicken burrito bowl, that God landed the notion of Cambodia on my heart out of the clear blue sky. Whether it was a twinkle in my eye that Brian saw, I do not know, but almost in mid-sentence he stopped and said, "Randy, if you and Krystal would like to get involved with this, it would be awesome."

I literally laughed and replied, "Well, tell me more because I'm intrigued." At the end of lunch he invited Krystal and me over to his home later that week to hear more stories and to see some photos from his recent trip to Cambodia. My world was rocked that day at Chipotle! Since then I have said many times, "Be careful about Chipotle! Your life can change over one burrito bowl!!"

When I got home from work that day I asked Krystal, "So, how'd you like to go and live in Cambodia for the rest of your life?" She had two words for me... "I'm fine!" Then, of course, she wanted to know what I was talking about. I shared with her about my lunch with Brian and told her that he would show us some photos later that week. On the way home after seeing the photos, I asked Krystal, "So, what do you think?" She said, "It's great, but I don't feel called to work with children." I replied, "Well, I don't either, but I'm not going to say that I can't be called." Later on, we found out that Brian would make a trip to Cambodia that summer (2009) and he invited us to go along to "scope out the land." We agreed and in June in 2009 we made our first exploratory trip to Cambodia.

We decided that the purpose of that first trip was to discover if there were any "red flags" that indicated we should not go to Cambodia. Both Krystal and I are of the mind that all Christians are called to "go into all the world" with the gospel, so rather than going and looking for a call (the call to go has already been given), we should go trying to discern if there was a call for us "not" to go. We discovered that it would not be a "walk in the park" for us to go and live in a place where there were only two other westerners. A place where there was no electricity and the only water was from a well on site, and where we did not know a word of the language. BUT we did not think that any of those things were deal breakers so we came home praying that God would confirm the call to our hearts once we got back.

Shortly after returning to Bay Area, I met with Pastor Larry Vold and shared with him what we thought God was stirring in our hearts. Larry's gracious response was, "Randy, we don't want you and Krystal to leave, but if this is God's call on your life, we would never stand in your way." With that amazing response we felt free to seek God's will to lead us forward. Finally, in October of 2009 we announced to the church that it was our intention to move to Cambodia in the summer of 2010 and stay for a period of at least two years. For the next 10 months we spent our time "untethering" ourselves from God's blessings. Then, in August of 2010, we got on a plane with the few worldly belongings we had left and headed out for Cambodia.

The rest is history, as they say, so I'll not go into detail in describing the amazing eight years that we lived and served in Cambodia. Suffice it to say, we had no idea God would provide us a lifelong "souvenir" from our years in Cambodia in the form of a little boy whom we named Noel. He came to us completely unexpectedly at the Christmas season of 2011. We named him Noel because the people who dropped him at the orphanage where we worked said they did not know his name. At the time we thought he was God's Christmas gift to the orphanage, so we gave him the name Noel. Now he is Noel Tum Dara Odom and he is a passport carrying American citizen. The journey toward Noel's adoption would fill another testimony so I'll save that for another time.

Apart from the generous and loving support of Neighborhood (3Crosses) Church, we would not have had the wonderful experience in Cambodia that we did. We thank God every day for this church! And we thank Him that the church was willing to open the doors to us again when we returned to the U.S, in the summer of 2018. I have said that it was like God said in 2010, "I'm gonna push 'pause' on your life here in the States and I want you two to go play and serve me in Cambodia." Then, eight years later, as we returned to the States, it was as if God pushed "play" again for us.

Though much has changed for us since we left the U.S. in 2010, coming back to this wonderful church has made us realize how much has stayed the same. Our God is the same yesterday, today and forever, and His people remain loving, generous and responsive to our presence in community. We could not be more thankful for that.

Key Scripture

In conclusion, I hearken back to Ephesians 3:20, which reads, "Now to him who is able to do immeasurably more than all we ask or imagine, according to his power that is at work within us, to him be glory in the church and in Christ Jesus throughout all generations, for ever and ever! Amen."

Truly, God has done "immeasurably more" than anything I could have ever asked or imagined. I give Him all the glory and I pray that this testimony of His goodness, faithfulness and power will encourage future generations as they consider how God might lead and use them in the service of His kingdom.

Redgy Jackson

Believe in His Name

I was divorced once and my second wife died, but my third wife is healthier than I am! Both of my parents have died and I witnessed my best friend dying before me in a street accident.

As a youngster of about two or three, I was taken by my parents to a church and Sunday School at 8411 MacArthur Blvd. in Oakland. It was probably at a Jim Voss electrical demonstration, at age 10, when I started my Christian walk.

After completing college, I worked at Lockheed for four years. The gas crunch occurred in the late 1970s and everyone had to line up for gas. That ended the housing construction boom, and I found myself without a wife, broke, and unemployed.

My Dad brought me back to California and I spent the next ten years in the Singles ministry at 3Crosses. Finally, I married, joined the church choir, and performed in the illustrated sermons and summer musicals.

Key Scripture

"God sent not His Son into the world to condemn it, but to save the world through His Son. Whoever believes in Him is not condemned, but whoever does not believe is condemned already because they have not believed in the name of God's one and only Son.

- JOHN 3:17-18

Richard Kalman

Life Instruction Manual

I am one of nine children born into a family where both parents were Christians. My father was a lay minister and one of my grandfathers was a missionary. I did not accept the Lord into my life as I grew into adulthood. I thought I could handle whatever good or bad came along with my own solutions.

The unfortunate truth is that I had not thought out or worked out a solution for how I could effectively deal with life issues. I wandered through life like most people in our world, depending on myself to resolve each day's problems. I personally tried to plan and run my life my way and wondered why so many things went wrong.

I failed in marriage and had many problems enter my life that I was unable to resolve in a satisfactory manner. Many of my relationships deteriorated and things I did to find happiness seemed to end in failure. Running around from party to party and drinking with friends left me very empty inside, thirsting for something of substance, but not knowing how to obtain it. It was apparent that a change in the course of my life was necessary.

By the grace of God, after many years drifting in this confusing world, I came to realize that when one encounters problems that are progressively more severe, one should chart a new course. I was blessed to have loving Christian parents and siblings who were a wonderful testimony for me to strive for in my life.

I decided to search my local area for a church and finally settled on 3Crosses, a church that was founded on sound biblical principles. I discovered that God loved me and had a wonderful plan for my life. But God demonstrates his own love for us in this: While we were still sinners, Christ died for us." (Romans 5:8).

As I studied the Bible, my "Life Instruction Manual," I found wonderful truths and promises and a way out of my dilemma. I read that man (and woman) is sinful and separated from God, and that Jesus Christ is God's only provision for man's sin. "For all have sinned and fall short of the glory of God". (Romans 3:23)

Through Him, I could know and experience God's love and a plan for my life. I further read that each of us must individually receive Jesus Christ as Savior and Lord. "For there is one God and one mediator between God and men, the man Jesus Christ." (I Timothy 2:5)

So I received Jesus Christ and turned my life over to him. On June 11, 1972, I was baptized at the 3Crosses by Pastor "Pop" Ruhl. That decision was not made on an emotional basis, and no earth-shattering changes came into my life right then and there. But spiritual growth began and changes in my life did follow. Each day brings new insights through the Word of God and growth continues. Sometimes I move forward and some days backwards. But overall, the progress is in a forward direction.

I look to God for solutions, drawing on his infinite wisdom as the creator of all things. He provides the answers in His way and they are always correct. In my new Christian walk, I became active with a 3Crosses Sunday school class and the Fellowship of Christian Airlines Personnel (FCAP) ministry, a world-wide outreach to airline personnel that has brought many aviation personnel to a personal relationship with the Lord Jesus.

Key Scriptures

One of my favorite biblical scriptures (of many) is First Corinthians chapter 13, also known as the Love Chapter. This was read to my bride Branka during our marriage ceremony in 1989 by 3Crosses pastor Malcolm Cash who, coincidently, was from my hometown of Akron, Ohio. That chapter lays out wonderful guidelines for how Christians should respond to others with love in our daily life. Additionally, I like Galatians 2:20 that says, as a Christian I am crucified with Christ spiritually and I live my day to day life in faith. Also, I John 5:12-13 is a reminder to me that I was at a crossroads as a non-believer many years ago and I am blessed that I now have a new life in Christ Jesus.

Roger Decker

I Know I was There

I am sure my walk with the Lord is not much different from many other Christians, but still unique in its own way. I was raised in my paternal grandmother's Christian home, not my parent's home. Along with my parents, my grandmother gave me a sense of love and fair play and doing what is right. However, when I was only eleven years old my father passed away, and so did my interest in the Lord.

Fast forward 43 years to when my wife Linda and I visited our daughter and son-in-law's church in Grapevine, Texas. On the way home from Texas, Linda thought it might be a good idea for us to attend Neighborhood Church. The first sermon by Dr. Larry Vold was good, but what brought me back the next week was a young lady named Tiffany Thompson who was singing solo on stage. It felt like God was singing just to me.

Fast forward another 24 years, and now I greet, usher, and facilitate a discipleship group. I love every minute, seeing Christian friends and meeting new believers as they search for their calling. I'm not exactly sure when the Lord came into my heart, but to quote a now-deceased Christian brother, Bill Libbey," when it happened, I know I was there."

Key Scripture

Some of my favorite verses include:

Galatians 5: 22-23, which reads, "But the fruit of the Spirit is love, joy, peace, forbearance, kindness, goodness, faithfulness, gentleness, and self-control. Against such things there is no law."

I also like 1 Corinthians 13:13, "And now these three remain: faith, hope and love. But the greatest of these is love." Nearing sixty years of marriage, I have come to realize that love is our most precious gift from God. If you can keep these in your heart, I believe it is what the Lord wants for us.

My favorite scripture, though, is Psalm 23:1-6. Even when I was not walking with the Lord, I always felt a guiding force in my life helping me to do the right thing, to feel safe in sometimes scary or uncertain circumstances. I always felt I was being cared for, and knew the Lord is in my heart and I am in His. And, eventually, I will dwell in the house of the Lord.

Sally Holt

I Made Him a Promise

My mom died when I was only eight years old. During school breaks over the next three summers, our dad sent my twin brother and me to Percy Crawford Christian Camp in the Pocono Mountains of Pennsylvania. There were three separate camps for adults, boys and girls, but there was also a common meeting and campfire area. It was there that each of us said "yes" to the gift from our Lord Jesus. The we returned to our home in Brooklyn.

Each Sunday Pop would give each of us a dime to put in "the plate" as we faithfully attended Sunday School at the Evangelical Church of Peace. We moved to Miami when I was 12, primarily for Pop's health, and joined the First Baptist Church of Miami, where my brother and I were baptized together. I joined the choir with my step-sisters (my dad had re-married).

Soon my new high school church pastor arrived. He was the relatively unknown Charles Stanley and what a blessing he was. After graduation I attended a university 500 miles from home, no longer in a circle of believing friends and family. Note: my tuition was a whopping $75/semester!

I spent the next four years as a Registered Nurse (RN) in the U.S. Navy Nurse Corps, with exposure to good experiences and new worlds. I moved to California and attende or examined many churches. Eventually, the Holy Spirit led me home to 3Crosses, praise the Lord! "Seek and you will find." - Matthew 7:7

Shared Advice

a. I think a common feeling in new believers is guilt. As I grew from teen to adult, I experienced this uncomfortable feeling often. When I went away to college, I confess I put that out of mind. My advice now is don't! God was very patient with me. Do what it takes to keep growing in the Lord and don't let Satan have his way. Charles Stanley has said, "It doesn't work when Satan is your defense attorney!"

b. We act the way we think. Make friends with someone who understands the Word of God. Speak with a Christian friend or pastor if you have questions or concerns. Exchange verses, prayers and encouragements. "Trust in the Lord with all your heart and lean not on your own understanding; in all your ways submit to him, and he will make your paths straight." - Proverbs 3:5-6

c. When you choose to believe in Jesus as divine Savior, accept his promises as commands. "Peace I leave with you; my peace I give you. I do not give to you as the world gives. Do not let your hearts be troubled and do not be afraid." - John

14: 27 Commit to nurturing your personal relationship with God through study, humility, gratitude and in prayer, as your will yields to Jesus in your life daily.

d. Forgive. "Carry each other's burdens." - Galatians 6:2, Colossians 3:12-15. God wants us to depend on Him. As humans we are weak. He knew that when he told us to bear each other's burdens. We may need to ask Christ to enable us to forgive as he forgave. As we are in a forgiven state, how could we not do the same?

Key Scripture

"For it is by grace you have been saved, through faith—and this is not from yourselves, it is the gift of God—not by works, so that no one can boast."

- EPHESIANS 2:8-9

This tells the why, the what, the how, the requirement and the exclusions. It motivates me to feel thanksgiving and to want to "produce fruit" by sharing. It is my prayer the reader will be blessed by also choosing to accept this "gift of God."

My Pop: An Original Promise Keeper

I Made Him a Promise
He knocked on my door
I opened it wide.
He stepped through the portal
And then was inside.

I asked His forgiveness
Did repent all my sin.

I asked Him to help me
To be a good Christian.

He said He would help me
All my mortal life.
And then He would give me
Great Eternal Life.

I'll always remember
His sweetness to me.
His wonderful face
That I did see.

I made Him a promise
That we'll never part.
I'll always love Jesus
With all of my heart.

Arnold E. Holt
December 3, 1949

Sharon Breedlove

Fellowship of the Unashamed

I was an 8th grader 59 years ago, when the big blue bus came from Oakland to San Lorenzo. A girl down the street had invited me to the Neighbor-hood Church and the bus actually picked us up at our house.

At an evening service, I learned what Jesus did and I loved Him for it. I didn't know much more about Him other than He loved me, and that's all I needed to know. I gave my testimony from the stage with Paul Travis, saying simply that I felt a hole in my heart without Him. I was emotional when I was baptized by Kenneth Backlund. This was before he left to start another Neighborhood Church in Chico. That was publicly my first step of obedience. Ken Backlund, Don Larmour and Ed Harris Sr. led our teaching, membership outreach, ski trips and other outings.

When the church moved to Castro Valley it's new name was Cathedral at the Crossroads. The church sent a bus to Basic Youth Conflicts (Institute in Life Principles) in San Jose for a week-long seminar where I learned that man has a Spirit (God-consciousness), a Soul (mind, will and emotions) and a Body (flesh). I also learned that sin is anything that separates you from God.

I soon learned that circumstances may not be appointed but allowed. God orchestrates and is sovereign. The first doubt and question about my faith came after living through a crime against me. Afterwards, I bought a snub-nosed .38 caliber revolver, which shot hollow bullets and left a large hole as it exited. Sargeant Agler from the Homicide squad explained that I shouldn't point the gun unless I planned to empty it. I was ready to kill anyone that attacked!

Where was God in all this? I figured that He didn't love me so I felt empty. But God was faithful. He showed me the way through people like Paul Travis, Eleanor and Leland Todd. He taught me to listen (hear) and learn regardless of what I felt. God took care of having the right people at just the right time. I learned this during a communion service where everyone sat in a large circle on the floor, sang acapella, and I cried. Paul said it was good to be so tender before The Lord.

I wanted to serve Him, so I joined Charlotte Bellig with the little ones on the "story rug" and then Ethel Fix and Millie Story took care of my teaching needs. I was seeking with my whole heart and needed to learn more. God involved me.

I read the Living Bible at the Oakland Welfare Department, and Psalms 18 became very dear to me. "When I was weakest they attacked...(through verse 19)...for He delights in me." I learned that knowledge "puffs up" where true wisdom comes only from God. I wanted to see the world through God's Eyes. A wise man, Albert Einstein, said: "I want to know God's thoughts. The rest are details."

My name was Sharon McKnight until 1978 when Paul Travis married John and I at the 1st Presbyterian Church. (Our home church was busy with Christmas.) I became Sharon Breedlove and John and I had two sons, nine tears apart. We dedicated both of them to God at a church ceremony where the entire congregation prayed for them and their future. Both boys came up through Redwood Christian Schools and wanted to reach others for Jesus Christ.

Matthew, our eldest, earned his way to Hong Kong and China as a Royal Servant with Reign Ministries. Elijah earned a scholarship to The Hope Home in Calcutta, India where he taught English and some math for more than a year. When the boys finished their around the world trips, Elijah stayed in India at The Hope Home.

Matthew returned to the Hope Home with Impact Ministries and became close to Dev Sarker, the founder. Matthew, his wife Debbie, and twin daughters Lexi and Anya found a no abortion country (there are only 6) with a storybook river house where they are learning to serve God. Now, in my 70's (60 years at Neighborhood) I have survived multiple surgeries, cancer, stroke, rape, robbery and I have been burgled 9 times. God never left me; He did not forsake me. Everything was orchestrated by God, all part of His redemptive plan to further His Kingdom.

Now I am the dishwasher for the Woman in Touch luncheons and their outreach for missions. I also get to serve as a hostess and collect written prayers and praises to be sent to Woman in Action. That's where ladies fellowship and trim used postage stamps for missions and pray over the needs of the WIT.

Key Scriptures

I have advice and scriptures for the next generation. Since God is with us always, He deserves our attention. Include Him in all your conversations. Don't leave Him alone, which brings me to a favorite verse, 1 Thessalonians 5:16-18: "Rejoice always! Pray without ceasing. In everything give thanks."

Philippians 4:8 taught me what was permitted to think about. "Finally brethren, whatever is true, whatever is honorable, whatever is right, whatever is pure, whatever is lovely, whatever is of good repute, if there is any excellence and if anything worthy of praise, dwell on these things."

"Greater love hath no man but that he lay down his life for his friend."

We love God by loving others. God will take care of loving us. We all have different gifts but all are "Others Minded." My adult needs were brought into focus through the Challengers Class and Pastor Butch Monk who I sensed loved God with all of his heart. He spoke my language and continues today and has my eternal gratitude for his faithfulness to the truth. I will make it plain to you if you fully obey the truth you have.

God is not willing that any should perish. He gave His Son to absorb our sins on the cross. What more could He have done?

The Fellowship of the Unashamed

I am part of the "Fellowship of the Unashamed." The die has been cast. I have stepped over the line. The decision has been made. I am a disciple of Jesus Christ.

I won't look back, let up, back away or be still. My past is redeemed, my present makes sense and my future is secure. I am finished and done with low living, sight walking, small planning, smooth knees, colorless chintzy giving and dwarfed goals.

I no longer need pre-eminence, prosperity, position, promotions, plaudits or popularity. I now live by presence, learn by faith, love by patience, lift by prayer and labor by power. My pace is set, my gait is fast, my goal is Heaven, my road is narrow, my way is rough, my companions few, my Guide reliable and my mission clear.

I cannot be bought, compromised, deterred, lured away, turned, diluted or delayed. I will not flinch in the face of sacrifice, hesitate in the presence of adversity, negotiate at the table of the enemy, ponder at the pool of popularity or meander in the maze of mediocrity.

I am a disciple of Jesus Christ. I must go until Heaven returns, give until I drop, preach until all know and work until He comes. And when He comes to get His own, He will have no problem recognizing me. My colors will be clear.

"For I am not ashamed of the gospel, for it is the power of salvation to everyone that believes, the Jew first and also to the Greek."

\- ROMANS 1:16

Susan Okamura

Do Not Fear

The first time I remember thinking about God I was around nine years old. I know now that it was the Holy Spirit touching my heart since I didn't grow up in a Christian home and no one in my family or extended family ever went to church.

Around that time, I began asking my mom about God, and my sister was interested too. My grandfather who lived with us off and on (he was a caretaker and worked on ranches), came to our house one morning as he usually did when he wasn't working. He brought my sister and I a rosary because we had been asking for one. We each kept it on our bedposts. To us, it represented God.

In those days there were door-to-door salesmen who came around the neighborhood selling household items and miscellaneous things. My mom bought us a set of little Bible books, of which I still have Book Four, "The Children's Friend:

"Pictures and Stories of the Life of Jesus." The copyright date was 1928.

Even though my family never attended church, my dad encouraged us kids to go. Down the street from us lived a Swedish family, so my sister and I would go to the Lutheran Church with their youngest daughter, Marie. At other times, I remember my mom getting my brother, my sister and I all dressed up in our Sunday best and my dad would drive us to the Havenscourt Colonial Baptist Church and drop us off. I remember we were early and the first ones there. Once inside the foyer, I looked up and saw a large sign that read "Silence. This is the House of the Lord." We then went inside the sanctuary and sat down in one of the pews before anyone else was there. My little 5-year old brother sat there dressed in his best Sunday suit, including a new hat. The kind usher came by and said "Son, remove your hat in church." We didn't know any better.

I entered junior high school when I was only 11 years old and there I met my best friend, Rosemary. We would spend the weekends at each other's houses and when we were at her house we would go to St. Cyrl's Catholic Church on Sunday mornings. I loved it! I started asking Rosemary questions about God and church, so she gave me her catechism book. I remember reading it from cover to cover. I wanted to know so much about God. As I learned more, I wanted to become Catholic and told my mom of my desire but she said no.

As time went on, my sister and I met a family with three daughters who moved in down the street. Sharon was the youngest and was my sister's best friend. I remember one day my sister told me, "Sharon says we have to be saved." We didn't know what "saved" meant. Sharon's family were Christians and they attended Oakland Neighborhood Church on 84th and MacArthur Avenue, not far from where we lived. They invited us to church and we went every Sunday morning and Sunday night.

After a few months, my sister and I decided we were going to answer the "altar call" the next Sunday night. So, on Sunday evening, March 4, 1956, as Pastor Bellig gave the invitation to accept Jesus as our Savior, my sister and I raised our hands, walked down the steps to the aisle that lead to the Prayer Room where Sharon's mother worked, and we prayed together to receive Jesus into our hearts. We were so happy that we had just become "Christians." That night I wrote in my diary "we gave our hearts to Jesus. We are now Christians."

As we became involved in Neighborhood Church, we began going to the High School activity on Friday nights called the "Hi Wy." On Sundays, Kenny Backlund was our Sunday School teacher. It was one of the best times of my teenage years as I learned so much about God and Jesus. My sister and I would sit on our beds each night and read the Bible given to us by Neighborhood Church together.

Sometimes on Sunday nights they would have a baptism service and that was my next step, but when I asked my mom's permission, she said no. I was 15 years old at the time and it wouldn't be until I was 36 years old that I would finally get baptized.

During my time at Neighborhood Church, I invited my best friend, Rosemary, to go with me and my sister to the Friday night high school activities. I also asked my grandmother to go with me to church one Sunday, She lived on the next street over from us and my dad drove the two of us to church that Sunday. As Pastor Bellig gave the invitation to invite Jesus into your heart, as he did at the end of every service, my grandmother raised her hand and we both went to the prayer room together where she prayed to receive Jesus as her Savior at the age of 65.

At the age of 20 years old, I married a young man I had met at the Hi Wy at Neighborhood Church and we were married in the Crimson Chapel. He was a Christian and had gone to a Christian Elementary School. As the years passed, we had two children, a boy and a girl.

I had begun attending Fremont Neighborhood Church when my daughter was two years old and that's where both of my children grew up. I started participating in Bible studies with ladies from our church and one day I saw an ad for Bible Study Fellowship, which was taking place in one of the local churches. I went to the orientation and joined the first class, not really knowing how to actually "study" the Bible but I was hooked.

I learned so much after that one school year I was approached to become a Discussion Leader. For the next several years, I went from a Discussion Leader to becoming the Administrator in BSF. This was one of the best times of my Christian life. I was then approached to be the next Teaching Leader, the person who gives the lectures after the discussion classes. According to BSF guidelines, I was to ask my husband for permission to accept this position. I was to receive one of the biggest shocks of my life that would rock my world when my husband said no. To make a long story short, my husband had decided to leave our marriage.

One of the times in my life that I have actually heard God's voice was after my husband had moved out. I had been praying on my knees every day and thinking about what was next for me and my children. I remember saying to myself, "what am I going to do?" Then I heard God's voice so clearly say, "I will help you."

After my divorce, there were some difficult times that followed. I confess that I drifted away from God for a few years and made my own (wrong) decisions and have had many regrets. But God is a God of second chances and in His great provision for me, He called me back to Himself, "I will never leave you nor forsake you." Some years later, I remember reading in the book of Joel and thinking of those years I wasted, and as I looked down at the page I was reading, these were the Lord's words to me, "I will restore to you the years the locusts have eaten..." Joel 2:25. I have carried that verse in my heart all those years since and He has restored to me ten-fold...no, one hundredfold to my life!

As the years passed, I was able to buy a condo and lived by myself after my children had grown and moved out. I had to live very frugally but always paid my tithes each week and the Lord continued to provide for me. I had a friend who was going to refinance his condo and told me I should do the same. I was fearful that I could even attempt to do something like that even though I had managed on a shoestring to buy my condo, but would give it a try. Again I remember driving to work and saying out loud to myself, "Lord, if you can hang the stars in the heavens and call them all by name, you are able to make this refi go through." Again, I turned to Isaiah 41:10 for the Lord's answer, "Do not fear, for I am with you; Do not anxiously look about you, for I am your God. I will strengthen you, surely I will help you." Needless to say, the refi went through with flying colors.

I have been praying for my family members for many years and the Lord has again answered me through His word. One time I was praying for salvation for my family members with my Bible open and I asked for a word from the Lord. I looked at the page I was reading and read Acts 16:31, "...Believe in the Lord Jesus and you shall be saved, you and your household." I dated that scripture 10/25/93.

In the margin of that page I have written over the years, those who have come to the Lord: my son baptized 4-2-94; my mom, 6/1/94; my son-in-law 12/17/95. And while praying over one of my favorite scriptures, Psalm 37:4, "Delight yourself in the LORD and he will give you the desires of your heart." The Lord once again answered me with my grandchildren's salvations: Harlie on 7/20/14 and Ben on 3/26/16.

While driving on my commute to work in Milpitas, I would pray for my day ahead as my job was very challenging. So many times I would read these scriptures over and over "...Do not fear, for I have redeemed you; I have called you by name; you are Mine! When you pass through the waters, I will be with you; And through the rivers, they will not overflow you." Isaiah 43:1-2 would sustain me.

I continue to use God's word, along with prayer, for every decision and task in my life. It has sustained me and spoken to me at every turn. Specifically, one time I was trying to make a decision whether to continue to work or to quit and take a long break. After pouring over the scriptures for days, the Lord spoke to me again. We happened to be driving down to southern California and I was looking out the window, thinking about my decision. Again I heard the Lord's voice, "You have a choice." Right then and there, I blurted out the words, "I'm going to quit my job!"

What I would like to leave at the conclusion of my life is that the Lord is Faithful! Faithful to His promises, faithful to provide for your needs, faithful to speak to your heart with his mercy, grace and affirmation of His great and awesome love. He chose me before the foundation of the world; how awesome is that! "All the days ordained for me were written in your book before one of them came to be." Psalm 139:16b.

Key Scripture

I want to pass on to the next generation, the wisdom of the scriptures. God has provided a book to help us live life the way he designed it, if we heed His words. And I leave you with this scripture that I pray sums up my life: "Since my youth, O God, you have taught me, and to this day I declare your marvelous deeds. Even when I am old and gray, do not forsake me, O God, till I declare your power to the next generation, Your might to all who are to come."

- PSALM 71:17-18

Epilogue

You are our letter, written on our hearts, known and read by all men; being manifested that you are a letter of Christ.

2 CORINTHIANS 3:1-3

This book is a collection of personal stories and experiences, told by many of the senior members of 3Crosses Church in their own words, in their own way. Most of us are in our 70's or 80's. Some of us are in our 90's and still going! Some stories are short and some are long. Some of us came to Christ early in our lives, others not until much later. Some had dramatic salvation experiences, others not as much. But these are our life stories, our life experiences, and we have tried to relate them as honestly and candidly as we can.

We hope you have enjoyed reading this book and learning a bit about who we are, where we have been, and what we have learned along the way.

Our stories are all different because we are all different. But in all our stories there is one thing that we all have in common: at some point in our lives Jesus Christ was made known to us and our lives were changed. When we say "was made known" to us, we do not mean that we just read or heard about him or attended church for the first time. We mean that at some point, different for all of us, we each had an encounter with the Living God that changed our lives forever. It happened differently for all of us, but it happened! We were made aware that we were separated from a holy God by our sin with no hope of bridging that gap by ourselves, but that Jesus was offering us forgiveness of our sins and newness of life, all made possible though His sacrifice on the cross!

It is, of course, one thing to hear or read this, but it is quite another thing to have it united with faith in one's heart. But something happened to each of us that resulted in us believing in Jesus with all our heart.

Jesus described it this way; "Truly, truly I say to you, unless one is born again, he cannot see the kingdom of God." Jesus went on to explain that to be born again is to be "born of the Spirit." Coming to faith and really believing in Jesus is a work of the Spirit of God and that is what has happened to us, and it is what all our stories have in common.

All our personal stories describe, in our own way, our coming to faith in Jesus, the resurrected Savior, and testify to the truth of forgiveness of sin through His substitutionary sacrifice on the cross and to the ongoing working of God's Spirit in our lives.

The word "testify" comes from the Latin word "testis" which means to "witness." To testify is to make a public declaration, a personal witness, as evidence, to a truth or fact.

That is what we have done. Our personal testimony is our witness to what the Living God has done in our lives. This book is a collection of our testimonies, a testament to the working of the Holy Spirit in the lives of ordinary men and women.

We pray that the sharing of our testimonies will be a significant source of inspiration and guidance for the younger generation, both for believing Christians, as well as for non-believers.

The primary purpose of this book is to share our testimonies as a source of strength, hope, and encouragement to younger believers in the hope that they would glean wisdom and guidance from them. The New Testament letters of Paul, James, John, and Peter all stress the believer's need for patience, endurance, steadfastness, faith and hope in the midst of all kinds of circumstances. Hebrews 11 provides the testimony of a "great cloud of witnesses" that encourages us to "lay aside every encumbrance, and the sin which so easily entangles us, and run with endurance the race that is set before us."

The examples and messages from older saints that have gone on before, and have run the race with endurance, and are now approaching the finish line should serve as an encouragement and inspiration for those in the earlier stages of their own faith journey. But make no mistake, our testimonies are not about super-saints. Far from it! Our testimonies do not hide that we are all beset with weaknesses, still struggle with sin, make mistakes, suffer setbacks, experience loss, pain, and hardship but our witness is that the believer can still be victorious in the midst of it all because Jesus is faithful to us. Our collective testimony to the younger Christian is, Jesus is Faithful. No matter what, He will not let you down. So keep the faith, keep your eyes on Him. You can trust Him. But also remember He is the LORD of Heaven and Earth. He is not our cosmic butler. He will do things His way, in His time, and for His glory. But we can remain confident through it all knowing:

God causes all things to work together for good to those who love God, to those who are called according to His purpose. - Romans 8:28

This has been our collective experience and our stories testify to it in this book.

If you are not yet a follower of Jesus, we hope reading our testimonies has stimulated you to look into the claims and promises of Jesus. You owe it to yourself to obtain a copy of the New Testament and read the Gospel of John. It will change your life. It too, is a testimony. It is John's firsthand account, or witness, of his experience with Jesus. John wrote down his testimony (John's Gospel) and said:

This is the disciple who bears witness to these things; and we know that our witness is true. - John 21:24

What was from the beginning, what we have heard, what we have seen with our eyes, what we beheld and our hands handled, concerning the Word of Life- and the life was manifested, and we have seen and bear witness and proclaim to you the eternal life, which was with the Father and manifested to us. - 1 John 1:1-2

John says, "what I am telling you is true!"

Read for yourself what he personally saw and heard and experienced concerning Jesus. John cites the many things he saw and heard—amazing things—including unheard of miracles, healings, and the crucifixion and resurrection of Jesus. All the things he witnessed convinced him that Jesus was the Messiah, the Son of God, and that the promise of eternal life was true.

He saw it, he believed it, and has told us so that we can believe it too. Why?

He answers, *"what we have seen and heard we proclaim to you also, that you may have fellowship with us; and indeed our fellowship is with the Father, and with His Son Jesus Christ."* - 1 John 1:3

He tells us all this so that we also might have fellowship, a living relationship, with God the Father and His son Jesus.

You can start this new relationship with God right now by believing and trusting in Jesus and the sacrifice made for you. Jesus promised:

"For God so loved the world that He gave His only begotten Son, that whoever believes in Him, should not perish but have eternal life." - John 3:16

"He who believes in the Son has eternal life; but he who does not believe in the Son shall not see life, but the wrath of God abides on Him." - John 3:36

"Thus it is written that the Christ should suffer and rise again from the dead the third day; and that repentance for the forgiveness of sins should be proclaimed in His Name to all the nations." - Luke 24:46,47

The apostle Paul also told us how: "if you confess with your mouth Jesus as Lord, and believe in your heart that God raised Him from the dead, you shall be saved." - Romans 10:9

We have written our testimonies, like the apostle John, to tell you that you too can have a personal living relationship with God... just as John did.... just as we do.

Place your trust in Jesus Christ today for the forgiveness of sins and the promise of eternal life.

Here is a prayer to help you.

Dear God, I confess that you are the Creator and Maker of all things and that you are holy. God, I confess that I have sinned and know that I am separated from You by my sin, and I am in need of salvation. I know that there is nothing I can do on my own that would merit salvation but I believe in the work of substitution Your Son Jesus accomplished on the cross on my behalf. I believe Jesus paid my debt by dying on the cross but that He was raised from the dead. So, Heavenly Father, in the Name of your Son Jesus, I ask You to please forgive my sins. Lord Jesus, thank you for your sacrifice on my behalf. Please lead me into fellowship with You. Lord, I want to know you. I yield my heart and life to you and ask that you keep me and guide me by your Spirit from this day forward. I ask this all in the name of Jesus.

Amen.

DreamCasters Publishing

Everyone has a story worth publishing. You have a wealth of knowledge, life lessons, and wisdom that the world needs to hear. Why not share it? A book can build your expertise, help generate leads and set you apart from competitors. Most of all, it can impact lives and leave a lasting legacy. You don't need to be a writer to publish a book. Just tell us your story and we'll do the rest.

We are DreamCasters. We specialize in turning dreams into reality. Contact rick@dreamcasters.world to discuss your dream.

www.ingramcontent.com/pod-product-compliance
Lightning Source LLC
LaVergne TN
LVHW050539160826
845677LV00011B/2096

* 9 7 9 8 4 8 6 2 9 8 9 6 7 *